GENERAL, YOU HAVE MADE
THE MISTAKE OF YOUR LIFE.

Walter E. Busch

General, You Have Made the Mistake of Your Life

Printed in the United States of America

Published by Two Trails
1108 Appleton Ave
Independence MO 64053
816-836-8258

Sola Dei Gloria
Sola Christus
Sola Gratia
Sola Fide
Sola Scriptura

Acknowledgments

Many people helped me with this research; so here it goes. Foremost, I must thank Judge Candida Ewing Steel for her e-mails, proofreading, and comments on mainly the section concerning Doctor Mudd, but generally as well. Also, the staff at Fort Davidson State Historic Site; former Site Administrator David Roggensees, Brick Autry, and Jack Mayes, who helped me find research. Particularly, David was instrumental in my formulation of my thesis. Two other people were Robert LaForte of the University of North Texas and Ron Smith, both of whom provided information from unpublished research. Then, I cannot forget all my proofreaders: Sandra Turner, Kate Massie, and Chris Triller. Another person I must thank I only know as Kate. She works at the Missouri State Library and without my asking, compiled the census data I used in Appendix B. Marilyn Price-Mitchell allowed the use of a family photo. Ann Ratliff took photos of the Pacific House Hotel for me, but they were not used as an older one was found. Thanks to all. I hope it makes interesting reading and corrects some errors regarding the General.

Walt
2004

Table of Contents

Title Page
Dedication
Acknowledgments
Abstract

List of Figures

ABSTRACT

When General Thomas Ewing declined going on Sherman's march, his adjutant and his wife both told him that he had made the mistake of his life. Incorporating an overview of General Ewing's life, this manuscript highlights his relationship with Senator James Lane, his imposition of Order Number 11 to depopulate four Missouri Counties, his legal defense of Doctor Samuel Mudd, his public defense of President Andrew Johnson, and his political campaigns of the 1870s. By reviewing the normal source documents and sources not commonly examined when writing about the General, this manuscript shows the traditional view of his political demise, which is commonly attributed to a propaganda campaign initiated by George Caleb Bingham, Missouri artist, to be wrong. Instead, Ewing's loss in 1879 can be attributed to other reasons. In examining these highlights, the key mistake he made in his life is explained.

CHAPTER I

THE MISTAKE OF A LIFETIME

By the time of his death in 1896, General Thomas Ewing, Jr., (figure 1) had played an important role in several of the nineteenth century's more interesting dramas. As Kansas blood spilled to nourish the seeds of civil war, he was a leader in the fight to admit Kansas as a free state. When tracks were laid to take the iron horses west, he parlayed the legal interests of the Leavenworth, Pawnee, and Western (LP &W) Railroad by lobbying President Lincoln. Ewing served as a party official in a fledgling Republican party and was rewarded for his role by the voters of Kansas when he was elected the first Chief Justice of Kansas. After resigning that position, he led a regiment of Kansas volunteers off to war. After participating in three battles, his superiors recognized his command abilities and promoted him to brigadier general. General Ewing then assumed the task of policing the Kansas-Missouri Border. While he administered that district, the Confederate guerrilla, Quantrill, raided Lawrence, Kansas. Ewing acted decisively by issuing General Order Number 11. Later, General Sterling Price led the largest raid of the Civil War into Missouri and attacked Ewing's inferior forces at Pilot Knob. Ewing's defense of Pilot Knob's fort bloodied Price's forces and rivaled the Alamo and the Spartan defense at Thermopylae. The subsequent retreat through mountainous terrain equaled any of Caesar's forced marches in the Gaulic Wars.

When the President that both he and his father loved was assassinated, he suppressed his personal feelings in order to defend Doctor Samuel Mudd and two other Lincoln murder conspirators.

He came to the aid of a beleaguered President Andrew Johnson and publicly supported him through the travails of impeachment. By the time he left Washington in 1870, General Ewing had become such a strong, well known figure in national Democratic politics, he seemed poised for a political office of his choosing.

Yet years later, Curtis Rollins suggested in an interview with him, "You might have been president of the United States, or, should I say now, an ex-president?" [1] Instead, the highest office he ever attained after the war was as a Congressman. What happened to dash the ambitions of this man?

Ewing never achieved his desire of high political office. While his military and political actions helped to shape the country at the highest levels of government, he failed to achieve his immediate goal, a Senate seat. Researchers attribute this to either an ongoing propaganda campaign against him led by the Missouri artist, George Caleb Bingham, or to his defense of the Lincoln assassination conspirators. However, the true reason rests in one major decision in his life. That decision led him to another destiny, which he could only realize after suffering a defeat at the polls.

According to the <u>History of Fairfield and Perry Counties, Ohio, Past and Present</u>, General Thomas Ewing, Jr., "inherited his father's comprehension, forcible brain, and excels him in forensic ability." [2] Ewing freely admitted that he was "inordinately ambitious" and had "few equals in mental vigor." [3] Plainly, the General's best attribute was his logical, methodical mind. An obvious weakness was arrogance. Having been born into a family with upper class values and having been told throughout his life how intelligent he was gave him an air of superiority. One trait that could be either positive or negative was his ingratiating manner. This mannerism was so evident that, during the Civil War, his troops nicknamed him "Jesuit Tom," solely based on that trait. [4] His opponents respected his integrity in philosophical debates. His orations stirred crowds. Yet, he lacked the public self-centered boastfulness of Senator James Lane that seems a necessity. Rarely would he leap into action. Instead, his strengths rested in his abilities to plan and organize, which lend themselves to back room politics and not to grassroots movements. These characteristics were described by the Honorable Benjamin F. Simpson as he recollected how Ewing compared to other early Kansas politicians:

> Thomas Ewing, Jr., did not possess the social qualities of either Stinson, McDowell or Parrott he was more reserved and dignified; neither had he the ever-bubbling wit and the ready learning of Stinson, nor the eloquent recitative powers of Parrott; but he did possess the most sturdy, massive and comprehensive mind of any man that ever lived in the Territory. But it required great occasion and intense excitement to develop his qualities. [5]

General Ewing was as contradictory as almost any other nineteenth century man. His views on race and slavery were typical of the times. Even the most ardent of abolitionists rarely suggested that free blacks should be equal with whites. Still, by the standards of the day he was a cut above the rest. While he sought profits in his businesses and did not mind working with slaveholders to achieve that goal, he scolded a congressman for speaking negatively against black freedmen by injuring the character of a people as loyal to the Union...who have suffered more for constitutional liberty then, perhaps, you have ever given them credit for -- and who, after achieving their own liberties, at the end of a protracted and impoverishing struggle, have not disgraced themselves by denying the freedom of the [Kansas] territory to any human being. [6]

Ewing did not mind if he received publicity or money in the process of fighting slavery either. When some anti-slavery men allowed a runaway to escape the slave catchers, they were arrested and charged with violation of the Fugitive Slave Act. Tom defended the men by arguing that the slavers could not prove they were the representatives of the legal owner (they were the representatives of the owner's guardian) and since the Fugitive Slave Law was a penal law the court had to interpret the guilt or innocence strictly. His argument carried the day and the case was dismissed against his clients. [7]

Finally, as a commander of an army he issued orders much like those of any abolitionist general that slaves of disloyal Missourians were to be freed and escorted away from their masters. [8]

To form a fair opinion of General Thomas Ewing, his actions must be taken into account, possibly more than his words. His words were those of politicians. He easily grasped the feelings of those with whom he was speaking. If he was not fired by passion for a cause, Ewing's conciliatory mannerisms and words could make them believe that he shared their beliefs and goals. For all his nineteenth century foibles, when forced to action, his deeds spoke louder than his words.

In 1864, Ewing's adjutant told him he made the mistake of his life by not going with General Sherman on his march through Georgia. [9] However, that was not a mistake. General Ewing's failure to achieve a high political office rests in a decision he made immediately following the Civil War, and not due to his war record, George Caleb Bingham's propaganda campaign, or his defense of Doctor Mudd

President Johnson. The decision can, in part, be explained by an analysis of his relationship with Kansas Senator James H. Lane, but not entirely. It might be explained by his loss of the 1879 Ohio Governor's race. Still, that is not the complete answer. Business pursuits led him to the decisive mistake of his life and adhering to his principles kept Thomas Ewing, Jr., from achieving that which he considered political success...a Senate seat.

Figure 1. Brigadier-General Thomas Ewing, Jr.
Source: Photograph No. NWDNS-111-B-4705
(Mathew Brady Studio); "General Thomas Ewing, Jr;"
Office of the Chief Signal Officer; National Archives at College
Park, College, MD

1 Larkin, Lew. Bingham: Fighting Artist. Point Lookout, MO: School of the Ozarks Press. 1971. Page 328

Comment: This book is a basic source for much of the fiction surrounding Thomas Ewing and as such is quoted extensively throughout to illustrate how a key remark in the movie, "The Man Who Shot Liberty Valance," was taken to extremes in the case of General Ewing. "When the legend becomes fact, print the legend!"

2 Graham, A. A. History of Fairfield and Perry Counties, Ohio, Past and Present. Chicago, IL: W. H. Beers, 1883. page 89.3 Castel, Albert. Civil War Kansas: Reaping the Whirlwind. Lawrence, KS: University Press of Kansas, 1997. page 26.

4 LaForte, Robert S. Thomas Ewing, Jr. Unpublished Notations, circa 1990. page 5; Laforte, "E-mail to Author." 9 Mar. 1998; Laforte, "E-mail to Author." 23 Feb.2000.

Comment: LaForte found the reference to General Ewing as Jesuit Tom in a period Kansas newspaper.

5 Simpson, Benjamin F. "The Wyandotte Constitution." Kansas Historical Collections 2 (1875-1880): 236-247. Topeka, KS: KSHS. page 243.

6 "General Thomas Ewing Papers," William T. Sherman Papers (reel 10), "Letter to Honorable Edward Everett December 21, 1859." University of Notre Dame.

7 Smith, Ron, "E-mail to Walt Busch 4 Sep 2001 Runaways. Comment: Ron Smith is a lawyer in Kansas interested in Ewing's business and legal career. This information is from part of his as-of-yet unpublished manuscript.

8 Official Records (OR). The Civil War CD-ROM: The War of the Rebellion: A Compilation of the Official Records of the Union and Confederate Armies. Version 1.5 CD-ROM. Carmel, IN: Guild Press, 1996.Citation: 1-22/II: 460 & 450. Neely, Mark E. Jr. ""Unbeknownst" to Lincoln: A Note on Radical Pacification in Missouri during the Civil War." Civil War History: A Journal of the Middle Period Vol. XLIV No.3,Kent, OH: Kent State University Press, 1998, pages 212-216. Comments The text of Ewing's original letter to Schofield is not found in the ORs. The order to free slaves of Missourians in rebellion was General Order No. 9

9 Hannahs, Harrison. "General Thomas Ewing, Jr." Collections of the Kansas State Historical Society 1911-1912, Vol XII (1912): Topeka, KS: State Printing Office. pg 280

CHAPTER II

A FAMILY FLAIR FOR POLITICS

...and Kansas became the battle-ground.
Thomas Ewing, Jr.

Although the 1820 Missouri Compromise established that state's southern border as the northern boundary of slave states (with the exception of Missouri), Congressmen continued to argue the imposed boundary for years to come. In 1854, as young Tom Ewing watched, Congress decided to allow the citizens of each new territory vote on the issue. Young Tom Ewing returned to college determined to complete his law degree and to seek his fortune in Kansas, the Kansas-Nebraska Act's crucible. He was already "intensely anti-slavery,--far more so than my Whig training would account for," and this debate planted the desire in his heart to be a part of the new territory's fight against the peculiar institution.[1] His interest continued as he studied law. In the autumn of 1856, he departed Ohio to begin his professional career in the Kansas territory.

He established a law practice in Leavenworth with his brother, Hugh, and quickly became immersed in politics. In a letter to his brother, he wrote:

> I have had the hardest winter's work I ever had-
> chiefly political. If no other motive had driven me
> into politics, a regard for our business interests
> would have done it.[2]

To understand Ewing's interest in both law and politics, more than his visit to a Senate debate must be considered. His family life must be briefly reviewed.

Thomas H. Ewing was born in Lancaster, Ohio, on August 7, 1829, to the Honorable Thomas Ewing and his wife, Maria Boyle Ewing. Thomas Ewing, of Scots-Irish descent, was a prominent Whig leader. The senior Ewing was a friend of Henry Clay and Daniel Webster, who once declared that Ewing was "the best informed man he ever met -- that he never conversed with him five minutes but that he was wiser for having done so."[3] Besides serving as a United States (US) Senator, the elder Thomas Ewing served in President Harrison's cabinet as the Secretary of the Treasury and in President Taylor's as the nation's first Interior Secretary. Some considered Thomas, Sr., antisocial, but "his mind worked on an elevated plane, leaving the impression that he knew little of the small affairs of life, but at the same time he could often tell a farmer more about plows than he could tell himself."[4] His strong will was evident when he resigned as Treasury Secretary because he believed that, after President Harrison's death, President Tyler betrayed the trust of the Whig Party by vetoing two bank bills that the Treasury Secretary had helped author.[5]

Maria was also strong willed. As a devout Catholic, she brought up all the Ewing children in her faith. Tom's sister, Eleanor, followed her mother's example throughout her life much to the consternation of her future husband, General William Tecumseh Sherman, who would describe her personal faith as "bigoted devotion to the Church."[6] On the other hand, young Tom was less pious than his sister, yet he still carried a mystical tome, The Imitation of Christ, inside his uniform during battle.[7] However, age seemed to change him. By the end of his life, his son described Ewing's personal faith in these words: "By mental constitution he was unable to limit Christianity to any denomination, but he believed in Jesus Christ as his divine Master and Savior."[8]

The family lived at 163 East Main in Lancaster, 200 feet east of the boyhood home of General William T. Sherman and one block south of future US Attorney General Henry

Stanbery's home. The federal style house, built in 1824, was the first mansion in the city (figure 2).[9] A few years before his death in 1871, the senior Ewing gave the house to Tom, Jr. [10]

Tom's brothers were Philemon, George, Hugh, Charles, and foster brother, William Tecumseh Sherman.[11] Philemon practiced law and served as a judge in Ohio. George died in infancy after living only one year and five days.[12] Hugh, Charles, and Sherman became generals in the Civil War. Sherman's father, a prominent Ohio judge, died early in Tecumseh "Cump" Sherman's life. His mother could not support all the Sherman children, so friends offered to help. The Ewings lived two houses away and Thomas, Sr., chose to help raise "Cump," as he was the brightest of all the children. The family took him in and had him baptized into the faith. During the ceremony, the priest, who did not accept Tecumseh as a good Christian name, christened him William Tecumseh Sherman. The Senator later managed to have him educated at West Point. Thomas Ewing, Sr., never formally adopted Sherman, but he became a full-fledged family member when he married Eleanor Ewing. [13]

Tom's sisters were Eleanor and Marie Theresa. Eleanor, known as Ellen in most accounts, became a strong willed, matriarchal figure. Prior to her marriage, Eleanor collaborated with Eliza Maria Gillespie on a magazine article to aid the victims of the Irish potato famine. The two also sold tapestries and raised money in other ways to help the starving.[14] In later life, Eleanor, an anti-suffragist, spoke before a Senate committee and voiced opposition to giving the vote to women.[15] Tom's youngest sister, Maria, was "distinguished in private life for superior culture and character." [16] Maria was educated at Saint Martins, Ohio, and she married Colonel Clemens Steele. [17] Throughout their lives, all Tom's brothers and sisters were active in public affairs or politics.

Politics must have left an early impression on young Tom. Certainly, his desire to attain political office had its have

Figure 2. The Honorable Thomas Ewing Home, 163 East Main, Lancaster, Ohio. The Federal style house was built in 1824 and today is privately owned. It was inherited by Thomas Ewing, Jr., upon his father's death. To this day, the house stands about 200 feet east of the General Sherman Home. Photo by author.

roots in his father's expectations. If such ideas had not formed earlier in his childhood, events at age eleven certainly would molded his future life.

In 1840, General William Henry Harrison stumped during his presidential campaign throughout Ohio and was a guest at the Ewing home, "where he was serenaded in the evening and made a short speech, from the front steps." [18] When General Harrision became the next President, Tom's father became the Secretary of the Treasury.

In his teens, Tom attended Doctor John William's High School, north of Lancaster, where many prominent families sent their children. [19] Ewing's life long friend, Doctor Seymour Carpenter, later recalled the year 1846 with Tom and his other friends:

> For recreation we had evening parties, at private houses, picnics to Mount Pleasant, riding parties to the Kettle Hill; and in the winter numerous dancing parties, in the "Tallmadge House" ball room...I can remember no more delightful year in my life... [20]

Ewing was tall with an impressive bearing, was popular, witty, and his "chivalrous regard for the feelings of his associates...made him a man in whose companionship every one took pleasure." At age nineteen he served as the secretary of a commission whose task was to determine the boundary between Virginia and Ohio.[21] By age twenty, he had taken a position as President Zachary Taylor's private secretary. President Taylor died in 1850 after taking office the year before, so young Tom most likely worked as his secretary for only one year or a little more. Interior Secretary Ewing left his cabinet post to fill a vacant Senate seat rather than stay as a cabinet officer for Millard Fillmore, the new president. Tom moved on also and spent the next two years working as a claims clerk in Washington.[22]

While he learned politics at the highest levels of government, family life carried on. Tom lived at Blair House, across Pennsylvania Avenue from the White House, with his father, the Secretary of Interior. The social life at Blair House impressed young Tom Ewing, as exampled by the attendees at Eleanor's May, 1850, wedding to Lieutenant Sherman. Henry Clay, John C. Calhoun, Daniel Webster and President Taylor were among the luminaries in attendance.[23] Despite these political contacts and his practical experience, he needed a formal education to begin a life in politics, so he departed Washington for Providence, Rhode Island.

Tom was the only Ewing son to receive a secular legal education. Brother Hugh and his foster brother, William, attended West Point, while his younger brother, Charles, attended a Catholic school. At Providence, Tom attended Brown University, but left to attend Cincinnati Law School in 1854.[24] He left school in 1855 without graduating. Later, after he was elected to the Kansas Supreme Court in 1860, Brown University granted him a master of arts degree by special vote. In 1870, Georgetown College in Washington, D.C., "gave him" a doctorate of law degree.[25]

Immediately upon leaving Cincinnati Law School, he began practicing law in that city, but was quickly employed by John Andrews, a Columbus attorney. Ewing inherited his father's forensic talents and demonstrated that fact in three patent infringement suits. His success brought fifty more cases from the same patent owner.[26] Having become a successful young lawyer, his attentions then turned to starting a family.

Apparently, Thomas Ewing, Jr., had many romances. Sister Eleanor wrote: "Tom has been in love several times. His latest flame is Miss Ellen Cox, who is no doubt forgotten by this time." [27] Tom had not forgotten Miss Cox, as they were married in Philadelphia on January 17, 1856.[28] Prior to the ceremony, Ellen, the daughter of a Protestant minister, converted to Catholicism, seemingly to the relief of his pious sister and mother. After spending a few months in Ohio, the newlyweds embarked for the newly opened territory of Kansas, where land speculation could quickly make an ambitious, young lawyer rich.

Carte de viste. Brig.-Gen. Ewing. Photograph found in London, England. Private collection of author.

Chapter II End Notes

1 Ewing, Thomas, Jr., The Struggle for Freedom in Kansas. Reprint from Cosmopolitan Magazine. Library of Congress #TMP91000420: New York, 1894. page 1.Comment: Several of General Ewing's speeches were published during his life, but this is the only autobiographical account he ever wrote and he limited to only a one month period of the Kansas struggle.

2 Kansas State Historical Society. "The Thomas Ewing, Jr., Papers" (microfilm edition), manuscript division, Kansas State Historical Society, Topeka: Thomas Ewing, Jr. [TEJ] to H. Ewing 3 Mar. 1858). Comment: Mostly business records. Very little source material for his military career.

3 Sherman, Ellen Ewing. Memorial of Thomas Ewing of Ohio. New York, NY: Catholic Publication Society, 1873. page 230.

4 Graham, A. A. History of Fairfield and Perry Counties, Ohio, Past and Present. Chicago, IL: W. H. Beers, 1883. page 97.

5 Notre Dame Archives. Thomas Ewing Microfilm Biographical Sketch, n.p., n.d.

6 Fellman, Michael. Citizen Sherman: A Life of William Tecumseh Sherman. Lawrence, KS: University Press of Kansas, 1995. page 363.

7 Porter, Lorie Ann. "Not So Strange Bedfellows: Thomas Ewing II and the Defense of Samuel Mudd." Lincoln Herald (1988): 91-101. page 93. Comment: Porter contends that Tom Ewing was religious and cites the carrying of the tome as an example of his piety. Evidence would indicate she is wrong. Hirshson in his book, The White Tecumseh, correctly states that Ellen Sherman-Ewing and her brothers, Philemon and Hugh, were very religious. Tom believed, but did not believe the Catholic Church was the sole path to heaven.

Incorrectly, Hirschson states that Tom left the Catholic church well before his father's death. If that was the case, why was his religion still at issue when he stood for election in 1879?

8 Clark, S. J. Record of Fairfield County: A Biographical Record of Fairfield County, Ohio New York NY S.J. Clark Publishing, 1902. page 477.

9 "Square 13: Historic District." Fairfield Heritage Association, n.p., n.d., n. Page.

10 Sherman, 105.

11 Porter, 97.

12 Notre Dame Archives Comment: An extensive collection of letters of the Ewing family. This quotation is from their biographical sketch

of Senator Ewing.

13 Fellman, 4-6.

14 The Twentieth Century Biographical Dictionary of Notable Americans, Volume IV., np. 1904. page 296

15 Matano, Lisette, ed. "Nineteenth-Century Letters: Madeleine Vinton Dahlgren" Women of Letters: Selections from the Papers of Women Writers at Georgetown University. Washington, D.C.: Georgetown University Library Internet Exhibition, Spring, 1998. <http://gulib.lausun.georgetown.edu/dept/ccspeccoll/w9c.htm> Accessed August 17, 1999.

16 Sherman, 127.

17 Ewing, Hugh Boyle. Chronicle of the Ewing Family. Ohio Historical Society Archives: private publication, circa 1870. page 15.

18 Bartels, Carolyn M. The Battle of Pilot Knob 1864. n.p., 1995. page 36.

19 Ibid, 37.

20 Ibid, 104.

21 "Death of Gen. Thomas Ewing." New York Times 22 Jan. 1896.page 9.

22 Kansas State Historical Society. "The Thomas Ewing, Jr., Papers" (microfilm edition), manuscript division, Kansas State Historical Society, Topeka. page 1.

23 Fellman, 36.

24 Ewing, Hugh Boyle, 14.

25 Price-Mitchell, Marilyn. General Thomas Ewing. 1998. <http://www.sandcastles.net/thomas1.htm.> 1998. Accessed Aug. 1999.

26 Clark, S. J., 476.

27 Porter, 93. Comment: Although Porter records Ellen Cox as converting to Catholicism, she apparently had no intent-ion of practicing that religion and became a strong influence on Tom's church affiliation.

28 Ewing, Hugh Boyle, 15; Latter Day Saints. "Marriage Record of Thomas Ewing to Ellen Cox, File Number 1760721." Family Search International Genealogical Index v. 4.01. <http://familysearch.org/> Last accessed: 29 Feb. 2000; Wedding Note: "General Thomas Ewing Papers," William T. Sherman Papers (reel 10), University of Notre Dame. Comment: Several conflicts exist regarding when Tom married Ellen. Dates of January 7, 8, 17, and 18 are all recorded in various biographical sketches. Hugh Boyle Ewing originally wrote the 18th in his family history, but hand corrected it to the 17th. The 17th is born out by a document in the "General Thomas Ewing Papers," the priest signed that he "married" the couple and dated it on the 17th.

CHAPTER III

BUSINESS FIRST

Securing an income was Tom's first concern. He wasted no time in establishing a law practice and investing heavily in real estate. After arriving in Leavenworth, Kansas, he formed the law partnership of Ewing, Denham & Company. Having failed as a banker, William Tecumseh Sherman begged Tom for a chance to work in his law firm. Although Tom knew Sherman had only limited training as a lawyer, he invited him into the firm and, in 1858, the two brothers-in-laws established the firm of Sherman and Ewing at the corner of Delaware and Shawnee streets.[1] Within weeks, brother Hugh left a law practice in Saint Louis and journeyed west to join his brothers. In 1859, the firm brought in an additional partner, Daniel McCook, and became Sherman, Ewing, and McCook, the only law practice from which all partners would become Union generals during the Civil War.[2]

The Ewing law practice experienced both good and bad times. Tom encountered his first failure during the panic of 1857. He had invested heavily in land speculation, and this "forced him to make desperate efforts to obtain federal subsidies for railroad facilities."[3] Early in 1857, Tom was elected to the board of directors of the Leavenworth, Pawnee, and Western Railroad, while brother Hugh became its president. Trying to make a profit from his part of the LP&W would be a major concern of Thomas's for the next decade. In order to profit, Ewing opted to use political leverage for the LP&W against the interests of the local natives.

Obtaining the lands of Native Americans was not a novel idea, but Thomas Ewing, Jr., created the model by which

Kansas would eventually be free of reservation lands. The LP&W needed lands belonging to the Delaware and, later, the Pottawatomi. Through Tom Ewing's manipulation, Delaware lands slowly moved into the hands of the railroad. Thus, for the next ten years, "treaty-making on the Delaware model was the name of the game, with trust lands, diminished reserves, individual allotments, alienation, and ultimate removal the logical steps to be followed in 'civilizing' the Kansas tribes." [4] Tom Ewing, therefore, created the techniques used to obtain native lands peacefully.

As with so many railroad enterprises of the nineteenth century, the LP&W's outstanding debts far outweighed any projected income. That ongoing problem worried Ewing, and it was his assignment as a board member and the company's attorney to solve it. Lobbying Congress repeatedly, Tom Ewing dutifully sought amendments to the treaties involving reservation lands sold to the LP&W so that the company could delay any payments they owed the natives. His actions kept the railroad from paying its debts on time and kept them solvent on paper. He succeeded largely because of his ingratiating manners, to which both the tribes and elected officials succumbed. However, that was not the only reason for his success. The LP&W board lobbied natives and politicians, according to the ethics of that era. As the LP&W attorney, he knew of payments being made for political favors. [5]

The waxing and waning of the LP&W's economic prospects forced Ewing to deal with various players on the Kansas political scene. Indeed, the history of the LP&W reads like a battleground of Kansas free state politics. Charles Robinson (figure 3), head of the New England Emigrant Aid Society and first Governor after statehood, received shares of the LP&W for unnamed services. Robinson was not, however, a silent partner in the railroad; in fact, he served on the board of directors until another politico, James H. Lane, demanded he resign in return for his favors. In 1860, Ewing wrote

Robinson from Washington, D.C., to "make up $10,000 to $15,000 of Lawrence property with which to secure aid from the rapacious lobby, which will never let the [Campbell railroad] bill go through until their hunger is appeased." [6] Fifteen thousand dollars of real estate was minor in the world of Kansas political favors. When the US Pacific Railway Commission investigated the affairs of the LP&W in 1887, they found a memorandum from one board member (not written by Ewing, but, as his testimony before the Commission and letters written by him show, he apparently had some knowledge) which showed 64,650 shares valued at $4,284,000 passed to various legislators, executive officials, and lobbyists. [7]

Late in 1861, Congress still had not ratified a treaty which would transfer Pottawatomi lands into the hands of the LP&W. Ewing needed the support of local politicians to secure the Senate vote; thus, he approached Senator Samuel Pomeroy, who had his own railroad interests south of the LP&W. The Senator was open to Ewing's suggestions that supporting the LP&W would benefit him as well. Ewing also had to obtain the support of Senator James Henry Lane (figure 4). Lane had no qualms identifying his expectations if he was to support the treaty.

First, Lane demanded positions on the LP&W board for two of his people, who were to receive stock and stock options. Second, he wanted land. Third, he demanded the railroad board desist from using its influence against him. Finally, Lane, a long time adversary to Robinson, demanded that Robinson and another board member be removed as directors. Ewing acquiesced. Before Congress ratified the treaty, Ewing pacified Robinson with several thousand acres of land for his inconvenience and Lane with 9,400 shares valued at $470,000. [8] Both Lane and Pomeroy lobbied effectively for the treaty, which was passed on April 16, 1862.

In no way did the ratification solve the financial problems of Thomas Ewing, nor was the LP&W the sole

Figure 3. Doctor Charles Robinson, first Governor of the
State of Kansas. This loose picture is probably one of many
Robinson sent Ewing to prepare his <u>Cosmopolitan</u> article in 1894
(KSHS, Robinson to TEJ 13 Feb. 1894). Source: Thomas Ewing,
Jr.,
Papers Collection, The Library of Congress.

endeavor of his Kansas business career. During the Colorado gold rush of 1858, Ewing wrote a guide book to through the area.[9]

He also engaged in criminal law practice. Yet, these were sidelines to politics and the railroad, for most of his wealth and interests were tied up in railroad stock and lands.

Ewing was, at least in one aspect, decidedly short sighted, which doomed the LP&W. When two railroad companies approached the town of Leavenworth to finance a connection to its east, Ewing actively opposed the town giving these ventures any money, as he thought Eastern financiers would eventually pay for the connection.[10] Additionally, he thought that the town could wait because the steamships provided adequate freight service. In that, he failed to comprehend the technological advance of trains over steamboats. Still, the town opted to support one railroad other than the LP&W with bonds despite Ewing's campaign. Later, Ewing formed an alliance with Missouri Congressman and future Democratic Vice-Presidential Candidate Frank P. Blair to support connecting a railroad from Saint Louis to Leavenworth, but his actions came too late, as opposing interests in Kansas City won that battle, making that town the gateway to Kansas.[11]

To make a profit, time and again, he turned to lobbying for amendments to the treaty and eventually to the sale of the railroad. The Indian land deals he made through the endorsement of President Lincoln in 1861 and '62 would have helped his financial situation, but shortly thereafter people began to realize the war would not be a short one, so investment money became scarce. Ewing stayed in close proximity to Kansas throughout the war, traveling between Leavenworth and Washington, D.C., as the railroad's business demanded. In 1863, the LP&W reorganized into the Union Pacific, Eastern Division, but that did not end Ewing's financial woes. Like Ewing, the new major stockholders knew the investment game of smoke and mirrors. At war's end, his finances were in shambles.

Thus he emerged from the war with a reputation that might have aided his political career in Kansas, but with his financial position so weak that he decided to abandon his opportunity. He moved to Washington, D.C., where he resumed his career as a lobbyist and promoter.[12]

In 1865, he still held Kansas real estate and was the chief investor of the Missouri River Railroad.[13] Additionally, the Washington-based Ewing law firm became the legal counsel for the Leavenworth, Lawrence, and Galveston Railroad in order to secure land patents.[14] His real estate concerns involved a partnership which obtained a lease to mine coal at Leavenworth in 1860. Unfortunately, the lease had been obtained from the Secretary of War, who apparently could not issue this lease, and it proved to be "worthless."[15] Another partnership, the Kansas City (Kansas) Town Company, was formed, with Ewing as a member and land owner, in 1868. The tracts of land held by the partnership formed the nucleus for Kansas City, Kansas, which was formally incorporated in 1872.[16] While his business interests necessitated his move to Washington (which still included work as an attorney-lobbyist for the Union Pacific), one additional reason for his moving was his own belief that his political career had no future in Kansas, and that opinion revolved around one man, Senator James H. Lane.

Figure 4. Senator James H. Lane and his Wife.
Source: Photograph No. NWDNS-111-B-5138 (Mathew Brady
Studio); "Gen. (and Sen.) James H. Lane, Kansas, and wife;"
Office of the Chief Signal Officer; National Archives at College
  Park, College Park, MD.

Chapter III Endnotes

1 Fellman, Michael. Citizen Sherman: A Life of William Tecumseh Sherman. Lawrence, KS: University Press of Kansas, 1995.page 66.

2 Clark, S. J. Record of Fairfield County: A Biographical Record of Fairfield County, Ohio. New York, NY: S.J. Clark Publishing, 1902. page 477.

3 Taylor, David G. "Thomas Ewing, Jr., and the Origins of the Kansas Pacific Railway Company." The Kansas Historical Quarterly, Vol. 42 No. 2 (Summer 1976): 155-179. Topeka, KS: Kansas State Historical Society. page 156.

4 Miner, Craig and William E. Unrau, The End of Indian Kansas: A Study of Cultural Revolution, 1854-1871, Lawrence, KS: University Press of Kansas, 1990. page 15.

5 Taylor, David G. "Thomas Ewing, Jr., and the Origins of the Kansas Pacific Railway Company." The Kansas Historical Quarterly, Vol. 42 No. 2 (Summer 1976): 155-179. Topeka, KS: Kansas State Historical Society. page 171.

6 Ibid 160.

7 Ibid 170.

8 Ibid 166 & 179.

9 Monaghan, Jay. Civil War on the Western Border: 1854-1865. Lincoln, NE: First Bison Books, 1984. page 109.

10 Taylor, David G. "Boom Town Leavenworth: The Failure of the Dream." The Kansas Historical Quarterly Vol. 38 No. 4 (Winter 1972): 389-415. Topeka, KS:
Kansas State Historical Society. page 404.

11 Ibid 408.

12 Taylor, David G. "Thomas Ewing, Jr...." page 177.

13 Miner, Craig and William E. Unrau, 41.

14 Ibid 127.

15 "The Coal Mine," Daily Commercial. Leavenworth KS: 31 Dec. 1871. Reprinted on Internet: Kansas State Library Blue Skyways http://skyways.lib.ks.us/kansas/genweb/leavenwo/library/metro/commerce.ht m Accessed 12 Dec.. 1999.

16 Cutler, William G., "History of the State of Kansas: Wyandotte County, Kansas Collection Books." Internet Edition. Topeka, KS: Kansas State Historical Society, n.d. page 12.

CHAPTER IV

THE BOLTERS

Had James H. Lane not existed, pro-Southern apologists would have had to invent him. He reveled in disorder. His voice was a clarion to discontented northerners. On several occasions, he faced a hostile crowd; yet, by the end of his speech he could rally them to his cause. From 1855 through the end of the Civil War, when tornado winds ripped through the political landscape of Kansas, he was not far from its eye. Albert Castel analyzed Lane as "a cynic who posed as a zealot, a demagogue who claimed to be a statesman.[1] To most, he became the Grim Chieftain. To Thomas Ewing, Jr., he was "the greatest humbug of the age."[2] Regardless of his personal feelings towards Lane, Ewing would vacillate between aiding Lane or working with Doctor Charles Robinson, since both were leaders of the opposing factions in the Free State (also known as the Free Soil and occasionally, Liberty) Party.[3] Many chroniclers of the Kansas struggle likened Ewing to either a willow in the wind between these two men or "Lane's political creature."[4] Despite such claims, Ewing sided with Robinson at the crucial times. The young attorney even took the lead in two major events in Kansas territorial history: the bolting movement and election fraud investigations. Indeed, the history of the Lane, Ewing, and Robinson relationships shows that the Ohioan prevented much of Lane's mischief.

Before arriving in Kansas, Lane served in the 1846 Mexican War as a colonel of the Third Indiana volunteers.

According to General Taylor, that unit "acquitted themselves creditably" at the Battle of Buena Vista.[5] That battle, followed by the Battle of Cerro Gordo, led to Generalissimo Santa Anna's defeat, catapulting the American General, Zachary Taylor, to national prominence and ultimately the Presidency. Taylor's victory also forced treaties on Mexico, which established the current southern border of the United States. Returning to Indiana, Lane began his political career and quickly became the Lieutenant Governor. In 1852, he was elected as the Democratic candidate to Indiana's fourth congressional district.[6] During his term, he voted to pass the Kansas-Nebraska Act, which voided the Missouri Compromise and allowed new states to decide if they would allow slavery.

When his term ended, he decided not to stand for reelection. Instead, he headed for Lawrence, Kansas. The Indiana emigrant began his life in the Sunflower State as a Democrat, but Missouri Democrats controlled the party in Kansas and did not welcome his help. By late August 1855, he immersed himself in Free State party politics.[7]

Not long after Lane arrived in Kansas, the territorial legislature held their first session, during which Free State representatives were removed from the body. The lawgivers also "enacted all the general laws of Missouri, modified so as to be applicable to Kansas; and crowned their work by enacting a complete slave code..."[8]

Shortly thereafter, the Free State party held a convention of their own. Ensuring that everyone knew of his experience at presiding over the Indiana senate, Lane was elected president of the 1855 Topeka constitutional convention. The Missouri-controlled territorial legislature and governor considered this meeting to be a treasonous act.

Within weeks, an armed conflict, known as the Wakarusa War, broke out between Free State settlers and pro-slavery men when a Free State settler was killed. Lane and Doctor Charles Robinson were active in Free State defenses and instrumental in arriving at peace terms with Governor Shannon, thereby turning him against the pro-slavery men.[9] Through the political maneuvering of these two men, the Free State men won a major victory with little bloodshed. An election, held four days after conclusion of the war in December, 1855, adopted the Topeka constitution, and, in January, 1856, Kansans elected the entire Free State ticket to future state offices.[10] When the Topeka Constitution was brought before the US House of Representatives, it passed, although it was eventually defeated in the Senate. Thus, the duly elected state officers never assumed their positions. As such, Kansas was destined to remain a territory for several more years.

On March 4, 1856, James Lane was elected as one of Kansas's United States Senators under the Topeka constitution, but never served in that post, as Congress refused his credentials. A rejected Lane made his way back to Kansas on a public speaking tour of the Northwest Territory (mainly through Ohio, Indiana, and Illinois) when border conflicts again erupted. On May 21, Sheriff Samuel Jones, his posse, Missouri Senator David Rice Atchison, and some federal troops entered Lawrence and arrested several members of the Topeka convention, including Doctor Robinson, for treason. The pro-slavery sheriff ordered the destruction of two newspaper offices and the Free-State Hotel. General looting by Jones's posse followed.[11] The sheriff had expected resistance, which would help justify the charge of treason, but the Free State men refused to give him that satisfaction. An informant told the Free State party of the planned arrests. That allowed them to organize and prohibit resistance by any member. The governor and proslavery supporters were still decidedly nervous, despite their success in quelling the rebellion, for two reasons. First, Senator Lane, who also had an outstanding warrant for treason over his head, was leading an army back into the state. Furthermore, John Brown and a gang of fanatics massacred pro-slavery settlers at Pottawatomie Creek three days after the treason arrests. Of the two threats, Lane's army appeared to pose the greater danger.

When Lane heard that the leaders of the Free State party were imprisoned, he sent Robinson a letter announcing that he was returning with an army to release them. The army consisted of northern immigrants he had guided through Iowa, Nebraska, and into Kansas (as federal troops had the Missouri River blockaded against free state settlers) on a trek later named the 'Lane Trail.' Doctor Robinson wrote back declining his offer. Instead, Lane's "Army of the North" attacked Franklin and other proslavery strongholds.[12] This episode of the border conflict culminated on July 4, when federal troops appeared in Topeka on presidential orders and dispersed the Free State legislature.[13] On September 5, Lane led "two columns of free-state men gathered at Lecompton to release prisoners."[14] Later, in his memoirs, Doctor Robinson credited the local army officers with great restraint in this situation. He considered their restraint vital to the Free State movement.[15] A local officer met with Lane and pointed out the gravity of armed conflict against federal forces. Lane backed down from the fight. A local judge then allowed the release of the prisoners after they posted five hundred dollars bail each. Eventually, the US prosecuting attorney entered a motion of _nolle_ _prosequi_ (discontinuing prosecution) against the alleged traitors. Thus, the battle for freedom continued in Kansas. Lane and Brown fought and killed men on the prairies, while Robinson, assisted at times by Lane, fought the political battles. During the next several years until Kansas became a state, the territory hosted many elections, constitutional conventions, and armed battles. Tom Ewing told the story of an Ohio politician who parodied the Kansas situation to his constituents:

> He told with mock gravity of our many governments there; spoke of the Lecompton territorial government, the Topeka provisional government, the Lecompton State government, the Topeka State government, and described them all as being in full operation, electing State,

territorial, county, township, and city officers under each government, and all in full operation at the same time. He said it brought on a general election every month, and a county, city, or township election every other day. He...[made] the prediction that the next generation in Kansas will be born with ballot-boxes in their bellies, like 'opossums; so they can vote whenever they want to! [16]

About the time Tom and Ellen Ewing entered the Kansas territory, the pro-slavery territorial legislature met and called for a constitutional convention to be held in September, 1857. When it convened, this convention created the Lecompton Constitution. The people had to approve the constitution before it became law, but the majority of settlers, who came to Kansas from the Northwest and New England states, would not condone slavery. Trickery had to be utilized. The legislators invented a plan to give the voters only two options. The first was for the constitution with slavery and the other was for it without slavery. Either way, the voter had to approve the constitution. Should the vote go against slavery, the current slave holders would be protected (grandfathered) from the new state's laws.

On July 15, 1857, the Free State legislature revived the Topeka movement and called for a new census and new elections. Again, Lane became a spokesman for the party. During the convention, a rumor circulated that Missourians were again planning to invade Kansas. The convention then called on Lane "to organize the people in the several districts, to protect the ballot boxes at the approaching elections in Kansas." Lane did not stop at protecting polling places. He quickly issued orders forming volunteer companies to protect the ballot boxes and to record the names of all men who refused to support the Free State Party.[17] Lane's troops were armed, drilled, and readied for battle. On July 23, the senior Ewing wrote his son, Tom:

> The movement of the Free State Party in Kansas is a strange compound of fraud & folly--Fraud on the part of the leaders out of the Territory, urging those in it to Treason, & folly in those who suffer themselves to be led... The free state party if successful effect a revolution--if beaten, they are guilty of Treason. A civil war is the necessary consequence of the movement...enter not into their counsel.[18]

Tom's father insightfully recognized Lane's misguided actions, as did others. Governor Robert J. Walker knew of the military organizations and looked upon them in disfavor. Likewise, the convention delegates, meeting at Grasshopper Falls, nervously viewed Lane's actions. The convention directed Lane to give the Governor his troops in order to insure a proper election. Realizing he had lost some of the support of the party, Lane changed his position from one of armed action to passionately recommending that the ballot box be given one more chance.[19] The convention closed with the Free State party endorsing the October elections. As the October ballots were counted, irrespective of fraudulent proslavery votes, the Free State party won a majority in both legislative houses. According to some historians, this election was the only legitimate election held before statehood.[20]

The proslavery legislature refused to recognize the October election and continued on a course to a December election on the Lecompton constitution issue. Early in December, Tom Ewing traveled to Lawrence to serve in the Free State Delegate Convention. Robinson, who had been elected Governor under the Topeka Constitution, was the convention's chairman. Lane served as a committee chairman responsible for drafting a resolution denouncing the Lecompton

Constitution. Following the committee's lead, the delegates decided not to participate in the December election because they considered it a "swindle, and that the people could gain nothing..." The election passed and the results were decidedly supportive of slavery.[21] This fraudulent election gave proslavery forces one more chance to have Kansas admitted to statehood with slave property rights intact.

The Free State Convention reconvened on December 23. The party's debate centered on the issue of voting in the January 4 election for state officers. At that time, radical followers of John Brown secured control of the assembly. They opposed working within the framework of the Lecompton constitution and many sought armed conflict. During the early hours of the convention, Lane was "absent-- non-committal -- crafty-sick"[22] The next day, a rider covered in dust walked into the convention hall and announced that he had just ridden eighty miles from Sugar Mound to announce that General Lane was "in command there, and a desperate battle was impending with the Federal troops." Ewing then "sprang on a table and bitterly denounced the statement as an obvious trick and fraud to control the convention." Unfortunately, Lane's handiwork had been done. It forced an immediate vote during which proxies were received. Although only sixty-five delegates were present who supported the radical position, seventy-four votes were cast in favor of refusing to vote in the January election. The conservative forces, led by George W. Brown and Tom Ewing, received only sixty-four votes.[23]

As the convention broke up, Tom Ewing gathered the conservative forces and had the vice-president of the assembly announce that those willing to "bolt the action of the convention would meet at Masonic Hall on Massachusetts Street, at seven o'clock that evening, to nominate a State ticket and organize the Territory for the election." As the bolting delegates assembled that evening, a mob broke into the hall and ejected them. Secretly, thirteen bolters then gathered in the basement of the Herald of Freedom newspaper offices, owned by George W.

Brown, where they nominated a state ticket. Each nominee had to pledge to the bolters that, should they be elected, they would do everything legally in their power to wipe out the Lecompton constitution.[24]

On Christmas Day, the Herald of Freedom went to press announcing the actions of the bolters and the reasons why supporting the election process was necessary. R. J. Walker, the newly resigned governor of Kansas, described preparing the paper for print:

> With the adjournment of the Convention, accompanied by Mr. Thomas Ewing, Jr., I ascended to the third story of the office, not stopping at the sanctum on the 2d floor. Taking a place at the imposing stone, with pencils sharpened in quantity from thence on by Mr. Ewing, and strips of paper at hand, commenced writing up the proceedings of the last two eventful days, and such other matter as would bear upon the forthcoming election. Without leaving my place for any purpose, I continued to write, and the printers to put in type the matter thus prepared, proofs being taken as galleys were filled, which were read by Mr. Ewing, corrected, and immediately put into form. And thus we labored until 4 o'clock p.m., when sixteen newspaper columns were prepared and in type. At 5 o'clock the forms were on the press, which was running at its highest speed.[25]

Next, Tom Ewing obtained as many horses and riders as he could and "dispatched them to all parts of the Territory, each setting out on his particularly designated route as soon as 500 papers could be printed...the most distant points being first supplied."[26] Tom Ewing had supplied "the sinews of war, probably not less than one thousand dollars" by paying for the horses and riders.[27] The bolters had only nine days to campaign "over a settled territory two hundred miles square, without a railroad."[28]

Robinson endorsed the efforts of the bolters and wrote several public letters to the four corners of the territory "begging all to work incessantly 'til the last hour..."[29] Meanwhile, Lane, who thought his people had carried the convention, suddenly realized that the bolters had strong public support. Robinson, who vented repeatedly against Lane, commented:

> ...[H]e soon found that the bolters' ticket was being endorsed by all the influential citizens and that it would be elected, even with his opposition, and he joined the procession. As he had no use for a minority party, whenever he found his malcontents and "Danites" were to be beaten he would join the conservatives.[30]

Young Tom Ewing wrote his father after the January 4 election and commented on Lane's disingenuous reversal of allegiance:

> He is the greatest humbug of the age--and a mischievous humbug. He got up the war in Southern Kansas to operate on the Lawrence Convention, & succeeded in defeating the voting policy there. He tries hard to make up with the bolters now, and admits that it was the true policy to go into the election -- even bolting in. But the bolters are hostile, & will kill him if possible.[31]

On election day, Ewing and three other men took up

positions outside the polling window in the town of Kickapoo, a pro-slavery village numbering a few hundred people, "and proceeded to count the number of voters who entered. As the day passed, Ewing watched "gangs voting as often as six times." When the time arrived for the polls to close, Ewing and one of his men voted. Their ballots were numbered 550 and 551. Two more people voted after they did. The final vote, including fraudulent ones, at Kickapoo numbered 553 when the polls closed. However, the fraud did not stop with people voting multiple times; the final tally almost doubled after the polls closed.[32]

Fraudulent returns, destruction of ballot boxes, and theft of returns did not stop the Free State party from winning a major victory. Under the proslavery Lecompton constitution, the Free State party suddenly held the majority of seats in the territorial legislature. Twenty-nine house members and thirteen senators were party members, while the pro-slavers held only fifteen and six seats respectively.[33]

The legislature met on January 4 at Lecompton and immediately adjourned to reconvene at Lawrence. Shortly thereafter, Tom Ewing arrived in the city to ask for a board of inquiry.

On January 14, 1858, Tom Ewing obtained permission to head a commission investigating recent election frauds.[34] The board immediately went to work and called L. A. MacLean, chief clerk at US Surveyor-General John Calhoun's office, to testify. Prior to MacLean's testimony, Tom Ewing wrote his father of the fraud he was preparing to investigate:

> Calhoun left for Washington today--fled. He would have been brought up for forging election returns, of which there is evidence enough I believe to have warranted a presentment. He is the instigator of all the frauds, I have not a shadow of a doubt. Henderson, one of his tools, who recently got an appointment

from Buchanan [US President], obtained the returns at Delaware Crossing in this County from the Judges of election there, avowedly to bring them to Calhoun, & changed the returns from 43 to 543--That fraudulent return would have decided Leavenworth County with 11 members of the Legislature, & that would have decided the Legislature. A prompt arrest of Henderson prevented Calhoun counting that return. He said he had not received it. Henderson said he gave it to him. The judges and clerks at Kickapoo, Oxford & Shawnee have fled from fright. Those at Delaware Crossing have, I think, been coaxed out of the territory to prevent the exposure of Henderson and his associates.[35]

MacLean testified that Calhoun had taken all the returns with him to Washington to present to Congress. The committee, however, did not trust McLean's word and had the offices of the surveyor-general searched. The search revealed no evidence of missing ballots.

After MacLean's second day of testimony ended, Ewing was met on the street by an unidentified man, who "handed me his revolver as an assurance of his pacific intentions."[36] The man then told Ewing an interesting story. On the night before the chief clerk's testimony began, MacLean buried a large candle-box under a woodpile near his office. The incident was observed by Charley Torrey, the janitor, who then relayed the information to Ewing's unknown man. As they parted, the man revealed to Ewing who he was as a show of good faith. Ewing kept his name secret for almost forty years.[37] In February 1894, Henry W. Petrikin wrote Ewing and permitted publication of his identity in the affair.[38]

Ewing used this information to obtain a search warrant from a local judge. Two days later, Walker and his posse of twelve "pounced upon the surveyor-general's premises early in the morning, dug up a buried candle-box from under a great woodpile adjoining the office, and before noon he rode up Massachusetts street...holding the candle-box on the pummel [sic] of his saddle."[39]

Acting Governor J. W. Denver and other territorial officers met in Judge Josiah Miller's office to witness Walker surrendering the candle-box to the judge. Once the box was opened, the contents consisted of "all the returns of the election for officers of the Lecompton constitution, which MacLean had sworn had been taken by Calhoun to Washington."[40] Moreover, the returns from the Kickapoo polling place had mysteriously risen from the 553 counted by Ewing to 995 votes. Oxford and Shawnee ballots had increased tenfold from their legitimate numbers. The Oxford ballots had names copied from a Cincinnati, Ohio, directory, including the name of Salmon P. Chase, Lincoln's future Treasury Secretary.[41] Delaware Crossing had 336 additional names attached to it in a writing different from that of the election judge. The fraudulent vote from Delaware Crossing had made it possible for proslavery candidates to hold the majority of Leavenworth County's legislative seats.

Who buried the candle-box continued to be a matter of speculation for Ewing until 1894. After recovering the box, he swore out a warrant for MacLean's arrest, but the clerk had already fled the territory (MacLean and Ewing would oppose each other in battle six and a half years later in the Arcadia Valley). Petrikin specifically named MacLean. A letter from Ely Moore dated March 1, 1894, exonerated MacLean and, instead, named a man Ewing refused to reveal in his Cosmopolitan article.[42] W. C. Ransom wrote to Ewing and blamed MacLean and John Sherrand for breaking into Ransom's desk, removing the returns, and burying them. Ransom also exonerated Calhoun in this correspondence.[43] Who was to blame? The only answer can be that the entire staff of the surveyor-general's office was involved in a conspiracy of fraud, whether or not each knew of the others full involvement.

Ewing's committee continued investigations into the various elections, including the one on January 4, 1858, which had fraudulent returns, but still gave the Free State party a clear victory and defeated the Lecompton constitution. The election frauds investigations concluded when Ewing traveled to Washington and presented the evidence to Congress. With the election of a Free State legislature and the exposure of fraud by the proslavery groups, the battle appeared at an end. The bill to admit Kansas under the Lecompton constitution died on the floor of Congress. This meant Kansas officials had to prepare yet another constitution to submit to voters before statehood could be considered. Unfortunately, rumors of the proslavery constitution's death were premature.

The legislature needed to enact a new constitution and called for another convention in the spring. With an air of excitement in his words, Ewing wrote his brother, Hugh, that he had been nominated by a vote of 22 out of 24 in the delegate convention to serve in the constitutional convention.[44] Lane presided over the constitutional convention until he voluntarily resigned because of "the prejudice [by the bolters] existing against him..."[45]

That assembly created the Leavenworth constitution which was signed April 3, 1858, and adopted on May 18 by a vote of the people. However, when it was presented to Congress, it did not meet with favor, even by Republicans. From the time Ewing exposed the election frauds to the May 18 vote, Congress had decided not to accept the Leavenworth constitution; rather they decided to bribe Kansans into accepting the old Lecompton one.

In April 1858, Congress passed a bill, later known as the English Bill, to admit the state under the Lecompton constitution. The bill offered Kansans a bribe of five and one half million acres of public lands for schools and another two and one half million acres for internal improvements, if they would approve the Lecompton constitution.[46] This bill and internal squabbling in the constitutional convention caused a perplexed Doctor Robinson to write Tom Ewing:

> What has happened?...When I left Kansas...all with whom I conversed agreed with me substantially in regard to the policy for the future, if admitted under the Lecompton Constitution, & I supposed that I agreed with you. But now you & they are reported as having differed widely & warmly. Who has changed? [47]

Robinson continued to remind Ewing that should Lecompton be forced on them, the Free State men were to stay their course: no proslavery Senators were to be sent to Congress, the legislature was not to be controlled by proslavery members, and the movement was to be conducted peaceably. He concluded by providing the allegory that what the Free State men appeared to be planning in his absence was tantamount to the Continental Congress seizing power and then handing the reigns of government back to the British. Apparently, the articles Robinson read in the New York Tribune told the story of how the convention wanted the legislature to adjourn permanently.[48]

Later, Tom Ewing explained the situation in Kansas to Congressman James G. Blaine of Maine. The delegates, Ewing wrote, wanted the legislators they elected to hold a session in which the lawmakers would pass an act "submitting to a vote of the people whether they would change the Lecompton Constitution and Government for the Leavenworth constitution, and providing that, in case they voted for the change the Lecompton should thereupon die..."[49] Free State legislators would simply walk out of the territorial assembly. In theory, the assembly would have been voted out of office if the Leavenworth constitution were approved and would no longer have legal authority to act. However, the walkout would have left the proslavery Lecompton legislators in control of both houses with the ability to act under color of law. This extra-legal body could then pass laws protecting slaveholders and also elect two proslavery US senators. The resulting confusion might result in the entire struggle for power to start all over again. The people Ewing blamed for this debate were the ones who "had come to the rescue when the rescue was at hand and some had fought the free state party while they were fighting the Border ruffians." Definitely, this is a reference to radical Free State members, but, more specifically, to Lane. Ewing concluded that Kansans would not approve the English bribe, and if that meant Kansas remained a territory, that was all right.[50]

On August 2, 1858, the Lecompton constitution suffered its final death at the hands of the voters. One year later, delegates (without Ewing) met and produced the Wyandotte constitution. Under that constitution, as war clouds approached and Southern states broke their ties with the North, Kansas finally was admitted to statehood on January 29, 1861.[51]

Between the time the people accepted the Leavenworth constitution and the day the English bill was finally defeated, an event brought Ewing, the young lawyer, into partnership with the Grim Chieftain. Ewing was employed by Lane as one of his lawyers in a murder trial. Ewing did not serve as the lead counsel for Lane, but delivered a key argument on the fourteenth day of the trial. The young lawyer had to justify a homicide.

The circumstances leading up to the trial started when Lane and Gaius Jenkins became neighbors on the outskirts of Lawrence. Jenkins, like Lane, was a leader in the Free State party. Unlike Lane, he and Robinson were friends and their supporters hailed from the Northeast. Jenkins went to jail on a treason charge at the same time Robinson did. Still, Lane and Jenkins shared more than a fence line and party affiliation; they both were hotheaded. In 1854, Jenkins built a cabin and sank a well. He later built a frame house and sank another well, which went dry. In the winter of 1855, Lane bought the first house from Jenkins.[52] Jenkins needed water and the well was near the Lane cabin, and he routinely entered the property Lane fenced. While Lane was away from home leading his "Army of the North" to Kansas, Jenkins seized the Lane home, the well, and tore down the fence surrounding the grave of Lane's daughter. According to James Christian, one of Lane's friends, not only did Jenkins tear down the fence, but he removed the girl's coffin from the ground and plowed over the area in order to leave no trace of the grave. A tearful Lane declared, "Such a ---- ghoul is not fit to live. If I was only certain that he dug up my child out of revenge upon me, I would kill him at first sight."[53] In 1858, both men met at the land office to settle the dispute. As reported in Governor Robinson's memoirs, William Brindle, the land office register, wrote that he had decided the claim in favor of Jenkins, although Lane then appealed the decision.[54]

About one o'clock in the afternoon of June 3, 1858, Jenkins, two nephews, and a hired hand named Ray Green, all armed with weapons, walked up to the gate surrounding Lane's cabin and the well. Lane's biographer, John Speer, recorded that they came "to drive Lane from his home or kill him..."[55] Green admitted to Sheriff Walker and others that they went to Lane's to "get water or fight," although he later denied the statement in court.[56] According to accounts mostly hostile to Lane, the story occurred in the following order. Lane shouted at them that he would kill them if they entered the property. Jenkins replied by pounding away at the locked gate with his axe. Lane shouted the warning two more times before Jenkins destroyed the gate. As the four men entered the property, Lane ran into his house, grabbed a shotgun, ran out onto the porch and fired at Jenkins, who was now 30 feet past the fence. The shot peppered Jenkins with one hundred pellets. As Jenkins fell to the ground, the hired hand shot Lane, striking him in the leg. Lane stumbled back into the house. A crowd gathered at Lane's house, while Lane's wife tended to the injured abolitionist. Several members of the mob wanted to lynch him, but Sheriff Walker controlled the crowd.[57]

Sufficiently recovered to stand trial on June 15, Lane stood before a three judge panel headed by Judge E. D. Ladd. The trial continued until June 30 and was covered daily by a reporter from the Daily Missouri Democrat. On June 29, the trial correspondent wrote a synopsis of Ewing's justification for the homicide. His argument presented Jim Lane as a man defending his life and home:

"Jenkins and his companions, with force and arms broke into the premises occupied by Lane, and that he was killed after entering the enclosure...They were more than trespassers; they were rioters...early British law gave the subject the right not only to stand, but to go out and meet the invaders and resist them, by threats, intimidation, or reasonable violence. If they then imperil his life or limb, he may kill them, not to prevent trespass, but in self-defense...It was the same reason that caused the enactment (Kansas Stat. p. 289; sec. 14) That the voluntary killing of a trespasser by the man in possession shall be manslaughter in the third degree...If then, either one of the party snapped a cap, fired a pistol, rushed on him with an axe, or did any act giving him reasonable cause to apprehend a design to commit felony...he was justified in firing (Kansas Statutes 237)...[58]

Ewing continued the argument by outlining eight important points in Ray Green's testimony. First, Ray Green testified that they went to "get water or fight." Next, all four men were armed. In particular, Green had a fully loaded revolver. Third, Jenkins entered the yard by using an axe. Fourth, Green testified that Lane retreated from the fence line when Jenkins approached with the axe. Fifth, Green denied in court making the first two statements to the sheriff during the investigation. Sixth, four persons, not related to either party, testified that two pistol shots proceeded the shotgun blast. Seventh, the pistol discharged as Lane's gun discharged.

Finally, Green told Sheriff Walker "that if his pistol would have gone off, Lane would not have killed Jenkins." Ewing concluded his attack on Green's testimony by declaring that it was not reliable because it was contradictory (but not perjurious). [59]

One key element most writers of this story fail to identify is that there were two witnesses: a Mrs. Mendall and a Gates. They also fail to state that Jenkins and his cohorts charged past the gate, leaving the water bucket behind. Yet, they went for water! The witnesses and others within earshot heard either the revolver discharge first or the shotgun. The point seemed irreconcilable, but not to Ewing. He closed his argument by solidly proving that the evidence supported a claim of self-defense.

"...This pistol was snapped once before it was discharged -- for there is a bursted cap on the barrel preceding the barrel discharged. (Green swore that the first time he cocked his revolver it went off; that the second time the cap snapped, and the third time the barrel would not resolve. The pistol showed that the first cap was snapped and the second barrel discharged. It has, however, been in the keeping of a violent partisan of Lane's --Rep [the correspondent's comments alleging that Sheriff Walker may have tampered with the evidence).

When was that cap snapped? It was before Lane fired; this pistol is your witness -- you cannot discredit or impeach its testimony, and on the unimpeachable testimony of this witness, who is not swerved by passion or affection, or new made memory or fear of law; who has not denied on the stand statements made on the streets. We claim that Gen. Lane fired in self-defense, and that he go forth from this court acquitted of the charge, which the evidence in this case has so singularly overthrown -- leaving to him and his children his peerless reputation, unsullied by a judgment of commitment from your honors." [60]

Although several counselors concluded their arguments

on June 29, the reporter only included Ewing's remarks in his report. The newspaperman excused himself to his readers by simply stating that the county attorney and the two other defense lawyers gave expected performances, mostly long and drawn out, although Colonel Young's performance for the defense was that of a "fine specimen of a Western jury lawyer."[61]

The court adjourned until ten in the morning on June 30. Later that day at four in the afternoon, Judge Ladd discharged Lane citing the government's "failure of 'probable' proof to show that the crime of 'willful murder' had been committed by Gen. Lane."[62] Still, Lane could not leave an audience waiting and proceeded to speechify. According to the reporter:

"He was grateful for the favor of leaving this Court a free man, and returned thanks for the justice rendered him. He however, felt from his intimate connection with Kansas affairs, and from the fact that the Court was of the same political faith as himself, that the action of the Court would be misconstrued, and therefore he was willing and desirous to enter into recognizance to appear and answer any charge that might be preferred before the District Court. If then acquitted before a pro-slavery judge, his enemies could not say that partisan feeling had aught to do with it."[63]

Before the trial, the egotistic Lane held fanciful thoughts of being President. His supporters had ordered large lithographs bearing the banner slogan: "The Sixteenth President of the United States" below his portrait. The Jenkins homicide eliminated any further thoughts of such a possibility.[64] Some claim that the murder bore heavily on his mind. Monaghan reported that he took up religion, publicly announcing his transfiguration in many small towns. One tavern keeper in Baldwin City warned a boy leading a horse team to a creek: "Don't water them horses below where they baptized Jim Lane." Yet, piety was not meant for James H. Lane. Before the end of the year, Lane's voice again echoed through the crowds and had turned the murder allegations to political advantage.[65] The hope

56

of Jenkins' friends of a true bill (grand jury indictment) issued against Lane never happened. Furthermore, Lane eventually won the water rights decision. Ely Moore reported to Doctor Robinson that the conclusion of the water rights case was against Lane, but when Lane became a Senator "he had the case reopened, and the Secretary of the Interior reversed the decision of the Land Office and of the former Secretary of the Interior."[64]

Before becoming the thirty-fourth star on Old Glory, the territory had to endure two more years of political maneuvers._ In May 1859, the state Republican party held their first convention at Osawatomie. Kansas politics had always been a local affair during the struggle for freedom. Few people cared about the national Whig, Democrat, or Republican parties. Yet, with the victory of the Free State party in 1858, allegiances began to realign along the national lines. By 1859, only a few die-hard Free Staters attended their party's convention. As the territorial parties dissolved, the main political struggles became whether the Free State men chose the Republican or Democratic party and who would be the new leaders of the party. Robinson was not an officer at the Republican convention and Lane had temporarily abandoned politics after the embarrassing trial the previous year. Although Lane was free, the trial temporarily placed his political career in limbo.[67]

While Lane and Robinson temporarily removed themselves from politics, Ewing immediately involved himself in the affairs of the new party. Ewing served as one of the vice presidents of the convention and as a member of the platform committee. [68] As the year progressed, the election of state officers was paramount in the minds of the Republicans. In Lane's absence, Samuel J. Parrott, the Republican candidate for delegate to Congress, was easily elected over his Democratic opponent on November 8.

On December 8, 1859, Kansans walked the worn paths to their polling places to elect the future state officers and gave the Republican party a sweeping victory. Two of the officers elected were Doctor Robinson and a young attorney named

Thomas Ewing, Jr. Reluctantly returning to the political arena, Doctor Robinson won the governorship by a 2,513 vote majority. Thomas Ewing, Jr., was also on the ticket as a candidate for Kansas Chief Justice. Ewing's opponent was Samuel A. Stinson, who received 5,396 votes. A victorious Ewing received 8,010 votes, which was more votes than any other candidate in this Republican sweep of state offices.[69] However, the officials could not assume state office, because Congress had not yet granted statehood.

Prior to starting his career as a chief justice, Tom Ewing embarked on another political journey. Abraham Lincoln's election in 1860 reinforced predictions of a coming national battle. War seemed likely, but many men thought the coming conflict could still be avoided. Thomas Ewing, Jr., and his father did not believe in slavery. Both Ewings abhorred slavery, as any decent Whig or Catholic would. However, they did not associate their repugnance with the national issue of slavery to the personal level by refusing to do business with slave-holders. Neither man would allow the slavery issue to break the Union apart. Both would protect the South's peculiar institution, if it meant preserving the Union. To achieve this goal, both men joined representatives of twenty-one states in Washington on February 4, 1861. Young Tom represented the state of Kansas, while the Ohio governor appointed his father to be a delegate from that state.[70] This meeting became known as the Peace Congress.

The congress, which was a last ditch political effort to avoid war, met and immediately selected a committee of one representative from each state. The committee, on which the senior Ewing was a member, was to propose solutions to prevent a war.[71] The elder Ewing vigorously fought, with his son endorsing his position, for the reestablishment and extension of the Missouri Compromise line.[72] This proposal would have once again prohibited slavery north of the latitude 36 ^{0} 30' from the Mississippi River to the shores of the Pacific. The delegates failed to support the measure when first presented, but endorsed it on the second vote.[73] The peace meeting continued for twenty-three days and recommended to Congress a series of amendments to the Constitution to preserve slavery south of the Missouri border. Although these proposals were initially favorably received by the public, southern and northern extremists had committed to another course. When the proposals finally came before the US Congress, the work of the Peace Congress failed to garner the necessary support to prevent the coming conflict.

While the Ewing's were busy in Washington, Lane actively campaigned to fill vacant legislative seats in Kansas. State officers under the Wyandotte constitution had been elected almost one and one half years before they were sworn in. During that time, several vacancies occurred. Lane wanted to insure that he had supporters in place when the time came for him to be elected to office. So, he traveled the state speaking for various candidates to the state house and senate. By April 1861, the time had come to elect two United States Senators.

The Republican party determined that one Senator would be selected from south of the Kansas River and the other from north of those waters. Before the election had taken place, the Leavenworth Conservative declared: "The triumphant result of the vacancy elections will make southern Kansas almost unanimous for Lane."[74] The Grim Chieftain's campaigning for other candidates had paid off, but the choice of a candidate from the north was still in question.

Marcus J. Parrott of Leavenworth and Samuel C. Pomeroy of Atchison were the main contenders for the seat. However, Chief Justice Ewing, too, was interested in the northern seat. The Robinson-Lane battle had become an ongoing series of traded jabs. As the time neared for an election, Robinson announced his support for Frederick P. Stanton of Lawrence, who ran directly against Lane in the southern race. Additionally, Robinson knew of Lane's support of Parrott and opted to oppose this combination by supporting the efforts of his LP&W business partner, Tom Ewing. [75]

Lane proved craftier in this political game. Although considered a favorite, Lane was shocked on April 1, when Stanton received more votes in the senate than he did. The senators were mainly Robinson supporters, while many house members owed their recent elections to Lane. Governor Robinson pushed for the US Senatorial vote to be separate actions of the house and senate instead of the customary vote by a joint legislative session.[76] Since the senate was not pro-Lane, Robinson's intrigues almost paid off. Lane needed senate support, as many Parrott men voted for Stanton.

Suddenly, the Grim Chieftain received the encouraging news that Pomeroy wanted to strike a deal. In January, Pomeroy had chosen to ignore Lane's offer, but, by April, he found he was short of votes in the house and needed to deal with the devil. Lane agreed to give Pomeroy nine votes from house members, while Lane received one of Pomeroy's senate votes.[77] Through this deal, the Lane-Pomeroy senators nullified the April 1 senatorial vote and proceeded to hold a bicameral vote on April 4. Parrott learned of the deal and turned to Ewing, who never had much support and was clearly a dark horse candidate. The chief justice then withdrew from the race, throwing his support to Parrott. The election seesawed in one long ongoing vote, during which several senators changed their votes more than once. In the end, Lane and Pomeroy won. On April 8, Senator Lane began his trip to Washington, D. C.

Politics in Kansas involved constantly adjusting loyalties. Tom Ewing wrote his father in January 1861 that Doctor Robinson was attempting to become the federal Indian Commissioner without ever being sworn in as the first governor. Young Tom fancied that this could help him become a Senator and could defeat Lane.[78] Yet, after the April legislative vote endorsing Lane, Tom Ewing traveled to Washington to work with the new US Senator to promote Ewing's business enterprises. Once in the capital, Lane, who had previously begun a relationship with Lincoln, determined to make himself indispensable to the new President. In this regard, both Lane and Ewing were very much alike; both men could be unswervingly loyal to the Chief Executive.

Rumors electrified Washington, D. C., in April 1861 as war broke out with the assault on Fort Sumter in South Carolina. Confederates were massing for invasion and the White House was to be burned! At the time, there was no White House security and no secret service. Indeed, common people were known to enter the building unmolested by guards.

The President had to be protected, and Jim Lane decided he would do it. He called together 120 Kansans, who became known as the Frontier Guard.

At dusk on April 18, Jim Lane and his men, armed with Sharps rifles and cutlasses, entered the east room of the White House to be inspected by President Lincoln and Secretary of War Edwin Stanton. That night, Chief Justice Ewing stood side-to-side with J. A. Cody, Samuel Pomeroy, and Dan Anthony. Over the next ten days until regular troops reinforced the city, Lane's army protected the White House, a Potomac bridge, and the naval yard.[79] Lane received national publicity for his actions and the gratefulness of a President who would endorse the Grim Chieftain's appointments "without even reading them," while Pomeroy and other Kansas representatives had to go to him begging for a handout.[80]

After the initial crisis subsided, Lane returned to Kansas and raised two regiments for the Union army. Impressed with Lane's ability to raise troops, on June 20, Lincoln appointed Lane a brigadier-general with the federal authority to raise volunteers.[81] Determined not to be only a figurehead general, Lane took troops he raised and some federal troops and began military actions. Senator-General Lane raided into Missouri, sacked the town of Osceola, and, according to General Halleck, occupied his time by "the stealing of negroes, the robbing of houses, and the burning of barns, grain and forage."[82] Lane continued his activities as a senator-general until February 1862, when he refused to submit to General David Hunter's command. Lincoln sided with Hunter, and Lane resigned his commission to return to the US Senate.[83]

Mischievous as ever, Lane picked up the battle with Governor Robinson. Somehow, Lane and his followers developed the argument that, since the governor was limited to a two year term and that a year had passed before Kansas had became a state, Robinson's office was due for election. A judge ruled favorably for Lane's supporters, forcing an election. Robinson refused to stand as a candidate again, so, in December 1861, the people of Kansas elected George Crawford as the new governor. The ongoing struggle between Lane and Robinson moved to the Kansas Supreme Court.[84]

Crawford easily won the election as he ran unopposed. Nonetheless, he had to apply to the Supreme Court for a writ of mandamus in order to force the state board of elections to count his votes and certify his election. In January 1862, Judge Ewing considered the case of <u>State of Kansas ex rel. Crawford vs. Robinson,</u> I Kansas 17. The case might have clearly seemed a decision either for Robinson or Crawford, but that was not the case. Ewing reasoned that if the position was taken that Robinson's term was over, then some of the legislators, who were only elected for one year's service in 1859, illegally took their house seats in 1861. That illegality would negate the actions of that political body. One such action was a vote which set November 4, 1862, as the next election date for state officers. However, another illegality would have been the election of Lane and Pomeroy to the US Senate.[85] In rendering his decision, Justice Ewing avoided being influenced by the fact that he needed the Senator's support for the Pottawatomi treaty. In that business deal, Robinson lost his seat on the board of directors of the LP&W.[86] Irrespective of Ewing's associations with both men, Justice Ewing adjudicated the suit "strictly according to its merits."[87] After considering the issues, Ewing ruled in Robinson's favor, which had suddenly, with logical reasoning, become Lane's position.[88] Later, Lane would attempt to have Robinson impeached, but that, too, would fail.

Before 1862 ended, Thomas Ewing, Jr., would resign his

chief justiceship to join a Kansas volunteer regiment. His business relationship with Robinson had ended on a sour note, but by the time both were preparing to write about the Kansas struggle, all certainly seemed forgiven. Despite Ewing holding the opinion that Lane was a "humbug," they continued to associate throughout the war. Both men cared greatly for President Lincoln and later for President Johnson. In their own ways, both cared greatly for the state which they helped to create. Yet, those points alone would not keep these men together. It was Ewing's obvious business needs which kept the men on speaking terms. Although their relationship was a business arrangement, it was usually strained at best. Even Lane's attempt, around 1864, to obtain an appointment for Ewing as the Assistant Secretary of the Interior was most likely due to two personal reasons: railroad business, and the elimination of a political rival.[89]

Although none of these men could control the others to any great extent, the team of Robinson and Ewing had much more in common than Lane had with either man. The story of the trio exemplified the struggle of radical and conservative forces within the Free-State Party. A portion of that story involved Thomas Ewing working behind the scenes to defeat radical maliciousness and the pro-Southern forces. Kansas benefited by Ewing's attempts to manipulate Lane and by his masterly maneuvering to elect a Free State legislature under the rules established by the proslavery territorial government. He crowned this victory by exposing the voter fraud, which forced President Buchanan's administration to desperately offer the English bribe. That failed to garner public support and finally killed any thought that Kansas would be a slave state. The combinations of Lane, Robinson, Ewing, the bolters, and other Free State men moved Kansas through its birthing process. Additionally, Justice Ewing ruled on the first attempt to subvert the legally constituted state government. While Kansas would not have been the same without a Jim Lane or a Doctor Robinson, it certainly would not have been the same without

Thomas Ewing, Jr.

Signature of General Thomas Ewing from autographed copy of his sister's book, <u>Memorial of Thomas Ewing of Ohio.</u>
Collection of the author.

1   Castel, Albert. Civil War Kansas: Reaping the Whirlwind. Lawrence, KS:University Press of Kansas, 1997. page 19.

2 Letter: Thomas Ewing, Jr. [TEJ], to Thomas Ewing [TE], 18 Jan. 1858. Kansas State Historical Society [KSHS] . "The Thomas Ewing, Jr., Papers" (microfilm edition), manuscript division, Kansas State Historical Society, Topeka.).

3 Robinson, Charles. Kansas Conflict. Freeport, NY: Books for Libraries Press, 1972. page 14.

4 Brownlee, Richard S. Grey Ghosts of the Confederacy: Guerrilla Warfare in the West 1861-1865. Baton Rouge, LA: Louisiana State University Press, 1984. page 115.

5 Stephenson, Wendell Holmes. The Political Career of General James H. Lane. Topeka, KS: Kansas State Historical Society, 1930. page 24.

6 Ibid 34.

7 Ibid 43.

8 Ewing, Thomas, The Struggle for Freedom in Kansas. Reprint from Cosmopolitan Magazine. Library of Congress #TMP91000420: New York, 1894. page 1.

9 Goodrich, Thomas, War to the Knife: Bleeding Kansas, 1854-1861. Mechanicsburg, PA: Stackpole Books, 1998. page 85.

10 Stephenson, 58.

11 Monaghan, Jay. Civil War on the Western Border: 1854-1865. Lincoln, NE: First Bison Books, 1984. page 56-59.

12 Stephenson, 75-78.

13 Cutler, William G.. "History of the State of Kansas: Doniphan County, Kansas Collection Books." Internet Edition. Topeka, KS: Kansas State Historical Society, n.d. 14 Stephenson, 80.

15 Robinson, Charles. Kansas Conflict. Freeport, NY: Books for Libraries Press, 1972. page 334.

16 Ewing, Thomas, The Struggle for Freedom in Kansas, 10-11.

17 Stephenson, 86-87.

18 KSHS, TE to TEJ 23 July 1857

19 Stephenson, 88.

20 Cutler, William G. "History of the State of Kansas: Territorial History, Kansas Collection Books." Internet Edition. Topeka, KS: Kansas State Historical Society, n.d. Part 52.

21 Ewing, Thomas, The Struggle for Freedom in Kansas, 4.

22 Ibid 4.

23 Ibid 5.

24 Ibid 5; Cutler, William G. "History of the State of Kansas:

Territorial History, Kansas Collection Books."; Stephenson, 92).

25 Brown, George W. <u>Reminiscences of Gov. R. J. Walker;</u>
<u>with the True Story of The Rescue of Kansas From Slavery</u>. Rockford,
IL: George W. Brown, 1902.139-140

26 Ibid 141.

27 Robinson, 377.

28 Ewing, Thomas, <u>The Struggle for Freedom in Kansas</u>, 5.

29 Brown, 141.

30 Robinson, 377. ; note: The Danites was a secret organization
within the Free State party leaders which initially included both Robinson
and Lane, but, within a year, had become a Lane organization. The group
was called Danites after the secret Mormon society of the same name
reportedly formed in 1838, and as such became a colloquialism for any
secret society.

31 KSHS, TEJ to TE 18 Jan. 1858.

32 Ewing, Thomas, <u>The Struggle for Freedom in Kansas</u>, 6.

33 Brown 145

34 Ibid 145; Ewing Thomas, <u>The Struggle for Freedom in</u>
<u>Kansas,</u> 8.

35 KSHS, TEJ to TE 18 Jan. 1858, 1.

36 Ewing, Thomas, <u>The Struggle for Freedom in Kansas</u>, 8.

37 Ibid 9.

38 KSHS, Petrikin to TEJ 23 Feb. 1894.

39 Ewing, Thomas, <u>The Struggle for Freedom in Kansas</u>, 9.

40 Ibid 9.

41 Speer, John. <u>Life of Gen. James H. Lane, "The Liberator of</u>
<u>Kansas."</u> Garden City, KS: John Speer Printer 1896. page 142-143.

42 Ewing, Thomas, <u>The Struggle for Freedom in Kansas</u>, 9.

43 KSHS, Ransom to TEJ 30 May 1894, 2.

44 KSHS, TEJ to Hugh Ewing 3 Mar. 1858.

45 Stephenson, 95; Cutler, William G., "History of the State of
Kansas: Territorial History Part 53.

46 Ewing, Thomas, <u>The Struggle for Freedom in Kansas</u>, 9.

47 KSHS, Robinson to TEJ 13 Apr. 1858.

48 Ibid.

49 KSHS, TEJ to Blaine 11 May 1858.

50 Ibid.

51 Stephenson, 95.

52 Robinson, 421.

53 Goodrich, Thomas, <u>War to the Knife,</u> 208; Speer, 214).

54 Robinson, 423.

55 Speer, 204.

56 "The Homicide At Lawrence: Fourteenth Day," <u>Daily</u>

Missouri Democrat, 8 July 1858: Page 1, Col 6.

57   Goodrich, Thomas. War to the Knife, 210;   Stephenson, 96; Robinson, 422.

58   "The Homicide At Lawrence: Fourteenth Day," Daily Missouri Democrat, 8 July 1858: Page 1, Col 6.

59   Ibid.

60   Ibid.

61   Ibid.

62   "The Homicide At Lawrence: Close of the Proceedings." Daily Missouri Democrat 10 July 1858: Page 2, Col 3.

63   Ibid.

64   Stephenson, 98.

65   Monaghan, 108-109.

66   Robinson, 424.

67   "The Homicide At Lawrence: Fourteenth Day," Daily Missouri Democrat, 8 July 1858: Page 1, Col 6.

68   Cutler, William G. "History of the State of Kansas: Territorial History, Kansas Collection Books." Part 56.

69   Ibid, Part 60.

70   Sherman, Ellen Ewing. Memorial of Thomas Ewing of Ohio. New York, NY: Catholic Publication Society, 1873. page 103.

Comment: This is a vanity publication by Ellen Sherman to honor her father. The book has several biographical sketches of the Senator as well as letters of condolence from family and friends. The strained relationship between Tom, Jr., and Ellen, is clearly indicated by the fact that he is the only family member who does not have a letter published in it, although he supplied some letters of sympathy that were addressed to him. He is also mentioned significantly less than any other family member. Ironically, the copy of Ellen's book I have is autographed by Tom, Jr.

71   Ibid, 190.

72   Notre Dame Archives. Thomas Ewing Microfilm Biographical Sketch, n. p., n.d.

73   Confederate Military History Vol 1-12 CD-ROM. Carmel, IN: Guild Press, 1997.

74   Stephenson, 101.

75   Castel, Albert. Civil War Kansas: Reaping the Whirlwind, 23-25.

76   Ibid, 31.

77   Stephenson, 102.

78   Castel, Albert. Civil War Kansas: Reaping the Whirlwind, 27.

79   Ibid, 34; Speer, 234-241;   Monaghan, 128;   Stephenson,

104-105.

80 Castel, Albert. <u>Civil War Kansas: Reaping the Whirlwind</u>, 35.

81 Stephenson, 106.

82 Ibid, 115.

83 Ibid, 122.

84 Spring, Leverett Wilson. <u>Kansas: The Prelude to the War for the Union</u>. Kansas Collection Books. Internet Edition. Topeka, KS: Kansas State Historical Society, n.d. page 284.

85 Ibid, 284; Castel, Albert. <u>Civil War Kansas: Reaping the Whirlwind</u>, 69-70.

86 Taylor, David G., "Thomas Ewing, Jr., and the Origins of the Kansas Pacific Railway Company." <u>The Kansas Historical Quarterly</u>, Vol. 42 No. 2 (Summer1976): 155-179.

Topeka, KS: Kansas State Historical Society.

87 Castel, Albert. <u>Civil War Kansas,</u> 69-70.

88 Ibid, 69-70; Spring, 284.

89 Miner, Craig and William E. Unrau, <u>The End of Indian Kansas: A Study of Cultural Revolution, 1854-1871</u>, Lawrence, KS: University Press of Kansas, 1990. page 40.

CHAPTER V

A LAWYER GOES TO WAR

After achieving the status of being the first Supreme
Court Chief Justice of Kansas, Thomas Ewing, Jr., remained
unsatisfied. His goal was to become a US Senator and being a
judge was not the same.[1] Being a judge, even the judge of a
state supreme court, was not a challenge to him. Being
involved in political debate interested him, but arbitrating them
after they occurred did not. So, it should not have surprised his
family when, on August 6, 1862, Judge Ewing embarked on a
military career, which he believed was a pathway to political
office. It was his decision during this period to join the
military, to accept promotion to general, and ultimately to take
assignment in Kansas, which led to Order Number 11.
Therefore, his little-known achievements which earned him
promotion to brigadier general must be identified, as they
allowed him to embark on the road to command the Border
District.

Thomas Ewing, Jr., was selected by Senator-General
James H. Lane to command one of the Kansas regiments he was
raising. Lane had the blessing of the Secretary of War and
President Lincoln to do so, much to the consternation of Kansas
Governor Charles Robinson, who refused to commission the
officers Lane recruited, including Ewing.[2] Ewing's appointment
by Lane authorized him to:

> ...recruit one regiment of infantry in the
> counties of Leavenworth, Jefferson,

Jackson, Shawnee, Waubaunsee, Pottawattomie [sic], Riley, Davis, Morris, Lyon, Greenwood, Franklin and Anderson - comprising nearly one-third of the State - delegating him full power to organize and officer the regiment when recruited.[3]

Since Robinson refused to acknowledge any of Lane's appointments, President Lincoln commissioned Lane's men.[4]

Judge Ewing established a regimental rendezvous in the area of Leavenworth and named it Camp Lyon after Nathaniel Lyon, the former Fort Scott abolitionist captain and the fallen hero who forcibly kept Missouri in the Union. Ewing was particularly active in recruiting his men. Kansas had already given ten regiments to the Union cause, and filling additional rolls could be difficult. Still, by September 14, 1862, Ewing filled his quota faster than most regiments. In one instance, Ewing stole an entire company from the 12th Kansas, which Lane's son-in-law commanded! Lane may have approved the transfer because of the closeness he and Ewing shared at the time.[5] It is much more likely that Lane wanted Ewing to be indebted to him as much as possible.

Aside from Ewing, several other men who would eventually play parts in national politics were commanders in the Eleventh. Thomas Moonlight, a future territorial governor of Wyoming, was elected Lieutenant Colonel, while Preston B. Plumb, a future Kansas Senator, was elected Major. One other person of note was Captain Edmund G. Ross, commander of Company E and a future US senator.[6] The officers began drilling the volunteers regularly, while Colonel Ewing spent his time gathering supplies for his unit. Unfortunately, the only guns he could obtain were antique Prussian muskets.

By October 4, 1862, the Eleventh was outfitted and departed to Fort Scott, Kansas. They marched one hundred and twenty-five miles to the fort, after which they had five days rest. Then, they received orders to continue to Arkansas. General

Blunt was campaigning near the Missouri Indian-Country-Arkansas border, and the 11th Kansas was to rendezvous with his forces. On October 13, 1862, the Eleventh crossed the Missouri border heading toward Newtonia. During the march, Colonel Ewing stopped to give his troops some target practice. The Prussian muskets were very heavy and usually were loaded with three rounds of buckshot topped with one .72 caliber ball. According to Private Kitts, the unit's poor shooting allowed Colonel Ewing to quip that they need not hit their target, since with such "light artillery" getting close was sufficient. On October 19, Ewing's forces met up with those of General Blunt at Pea Ridge, Arkansas.[7]

From Pea Ridge, Blunt moved into Indian Territory and, on October 22, attacked Confederate forces under Colonel Douglas Cooper at Old Fort Wayne, but the 11th Kansas was not there. Colonel Ewing wanted this to be his regiment's baptism of fire, but the battle lasted only an hour. Ewing became upset when his Eleventh, who had to march to the battle, was left behind by their divisional commander, Colonel William F. Cloud, who rode out with his cavalry.[8] As the Eleventh arrived on the scene, the Confederates were in retreat. The baptism of fire had to wait.

For the next month, the Eleventh camped approximately six miles south of Bentonville, Arkansas, regularly foraging throughout the countryside. Then, Confederate General John S. Marmaduke and Colonel Joseph O. (JO) Shelby, who refused to surrender after the war and led his troops to Mexico, moved toward Cane Hill. On November 28, Blunt moved his men into position. As the fighting erupted, Blunt requested reinforcements. Once again, Colonel Cloud's cavalry rode past the marching Eleventh. Ewing then ordered the march "at quick and double quick steps" and kept this pace for several miles until they arrived at the scene.[9]

Blunt's attack caused the rebels to protect their supply train by a retreating, delaying action. When Colonel Shelby fell back into a good defensive position, he established a perimeter on Cove Creek and his units repulsed a determined attack. At day's end, the Union forces retired to Cane Hill and the Rebel forces to Van Buren. The Eleventh had received its baptism of fire and suffered its first casualties, but by all accounts served bravely.[10] In a letter to his wife, Ewing, however, expressed his consternation with Cloud's treatment of his unit in this battle:

> "My regiment was nearly run to death, going incessantly from 5 a.m. to 9 p.m., and travelling [sic] full 35 miles with their blankets on their backs--and yet Cloud complained of them for not outracing the cavalry which kept the road during the fight while we struggled through the brush for ten miles--the puppy!"[11]

After the battle, some of Captain Ross's men found a printing press and printed a newspaper, Buck and Ball, detailing their trip from Kansas. Yet, the war and General Blunt did not give them much time to relax or write. General Blunt knew the Confederate forces had more manpower than he, but despite his superior's repeated suggestions to withdraw, he decided to force an engagement. From December 4 through 6, 1862, the Eleventh fought minor skirmishes in the Boston Mountains and at Reed's Mountain.[12] Come nightfall on the sixth, Blunt knew a major Confederate force was approaching and, against orders, readied for battle. To save Blunt's forces, Union troops under General Francis J. Herron had to race from Springfield, Missouri.[13]

On December 7, 1862, 8,000 Bluecoats under the command of Herron met 11,000 Butternuts under General Thomas C. Hindman at Prairie Grove. Herron opened up the battle with artillery, but Hindman's plan was to flank both Herron and Blunt prior to Blunt's arrival, crush Herron and then Blunt. Herron's troops upset this plan by holding on until Blunt's units arrived around 2:00 PM. The battle continued until dark when the Confederates retreated into the Boston Mountains.[14] Each side claimed victory, although both lost over

72

fifteen percent of their men. This battle "was a brutal slugging match in which two armies traded direct frontal assaults until they were exhausted." [15] Prairie Grove could have made or broken an officer

Ewing was cited by Colonel William Weer, Colonel William Cloud, and General Blunt for gallantry, but what actions were remembered a few months later when he was promoted to brigadier general? One comment from Colonel Cloud suggested that Ewing had the ability to evaluate the battlefield situation. Cloud reported: "Colonel Ewing, anticipating my order, retired his command just in time to save it from a heavy flank movement." [16]

During the battle, Colonel Ewing split his command in half to each side of an artillery battery. Then, General Blunt ordered him to move forward with part of the 13th Regiment to his right. About 600 yards from the battery, they encountered fire from rebels protected by the crest of a hill. Union cannoneers brought forward two howitzers and began firing. The rebels dispersed. When the artillerymen ran out of ammunition, the Confederates began firing again. About an hour into the fire fight, Colonel Ewing noticed that Blunt's First Indian Regiment had broken ranks and were fleeing the field. He had that information relayed to Colonel Weer.

Five minutes later, his units were ordered to advance with the 13th Kansas and three companies of the 2nd Kansas. As Ewing's troops neared the hills crest, rebels charged over the top, firing on Ewing's left and front. Ewing stated that his command steadied, stood their ground and discharged four volleys. The 2nd Kansas had already retreated, and now the rebs threatened to surround his command. Ewing then ordered a withdrawal and his men did so, firing as they successfully disengaged from the enemy. Next, he attempted to form up resistance on a road, but the enemy was too close. After another disengagement, he managed to reform his troops around a fence row and continued to battle for "three-quarters of an hour, hotly engaged with the enemy." [17] Colonel Ewing had led

291 men into a battle, which Colonel Cloud considered "the thickest of the fight and staid [sic] there until, by order or necessity, the whole line fell back to more effective positions."[18] Ewing's column's losses (Moonlight and Plumb commanded two other groups of the Eleventh during the battle and filed separate reports) were "3 killed, and 3 mortally, 12 severely, and 11 slightly, wounded."[19]

After the battle, Colonel Cloud, who had been a preacher before the war, caught some men from the Eleventh returning to camp carrying a hog and some chickens. The next day the farmer complained to Cloud, who immediately issued a directive to Ewing to have the farmer identify the men and their officer in charge for punishment. Ewing used his legal skills to exonerate the soldiers by identifying the officer who ordered the pillage as the wagon master. By a previous order of General Blunt, the wagon master in the Army of the Frontier could direct the confiscation of property. An exasperated Colonel Cloud wrote to his crafty subordinate, "Your skill in clearing your foragers is commended...When I charge men with straggling and marauding, I propose to sustain the same, especially with an eye witness."[20] Cloud later reprimanded his subordinate once again when Ewing ordered his troops to confiscate any good mules they came across.[21]

Between December 27 and 31, the Eleventh campaigned with General Blunt south to Van Buren, Arkansas.[22] On January 20, 1863, Ewing was directed to take charge of the first 100 wagons, along with his command, and move to winter quarters near Springfield, Missouri, by crossing a swift, swollen White River.[23] The regimental history summarized this crossing:

> White River, the most considerable stream
> in northern Arkansas, was to be crossed, and
> it was very high and the current rapid.
> There were neither bridges, ferries, or
> pontoon trains. While the Division
> commander [Cloud] was exhausting his

ingenuity in fruitless expedients, Col Ewing
made a detail of competent men from the
11th, procured lumber and a cable chain
from a neighboring mill, and in ten hours
time built a first class ferry boat, that took
the army over swiftly without loss.[24]

On March 16, 1863, the regiment received a dispatch
from Washington, D.C., that Thomas Ewing had been promoted
to Brigadier General.[25] Three days earlier, Senator Lane
recommended to Lincoln that he place Ewing's name in
nomination before the Senate as a brigadier general.[26] While
his bravery and gallantry in battle were cited as the reasons for
his promotion, neither was the main reason. Colonel Ewing
had, in a few month's time, developed a first class fighting unit.
The Eleventh had brave, competent commanders, who worked
long hours drilling the men before their first march. In one of
the roughest battles in the Trans-Mississippi, Colonel Ewing
not only kept his unit in the thick of battle when other units
broke and ran, but he conducted an orderly disengagement.
At Prairie Grove and during the trek across White River,
Colonel Ewing displayed four traits that he would exhibit time
and again in his military career. First, his men had confidence
in him which enabled him to keep his command intact,
especially in retreat when it is so easy for men to fall out from
the ranks. Second, he could observe the changing situation and
find an appropriate action. Third, his good planning overcame
obstacles. Finally, he knew how to obediently follow orders
during battle. His promotion to brigadier general was therefore
as much for the display of these characteristics as for bravery.
After the Senate received Lincoln's nomination, they
confirmed it in a half an hour. However, while others,
including Lane, thought Ewing had command ability, his father
did not. In the past the entire family fought to obtain a proper
rank for Sherman and in the next few years the family would
lobby for Hugh and Charley to receive promotions. They never

did so for Tom. When the old Senator learned of Lincoln's nomination, he asked the President why he would do that for "the brat."[27]

On April 26, 1863, General Thomas Ewing issued General Order Number 1 from Camp Jewell in Vernon County, Missouri, assuming command of the First Division of the Army of the Frontier.[28] However, a new assignment awaited which would tax all his command abilities.

Chapter V Endnotes

1 Bartels, Carolyn M. The Battle of Pilot Knob 1864. n.p., 1995. page 23.

2 Castel, Albert. Civil War Kansas: Reaping the Whirlwind. Lawrence, KS: University Press of Kansas, 1997. page 88.

3 Burke, W.S., ed. Official Military History of Kansas Regiments. Ottawa, KS: Kansas Heritage Press, n.d. page 322.

4 Stanton, Edwin M. "Colonel's Commission Letter to Thomas Ewing dated 5 Nov. 1862." "The Thomas Ewing, Jr., Papers" (microfilm edition), manuscript division. Topeka, KS: KSHS.

5 Hannahs, Harrison. "General Thomas Ewing, Jr." Collections of the Kansas State Historical Society 1911-1912, Vol XII (1912): Topeka, KS: State Printing Office. page 277.

6 Burke, 323.

7 Scott, Kim Allen. The Fighting Printers of Company E. Johnson, AR: Kinnally Press, 1987, page 7.

8 Scott, Kim Allen. "The Preacher, the Lawyer, and the Spoils of War." Kansas History Vol. 13 No.4 (1990): 206-217. Topeka, KS: Kansas State Historical Society. page 210; Civil War Sites Advisory Commission. "Old Fort Wayne Battle Summary." Civil War Sites Advisory Commission Report on the Nation's Civil War Battlefields Technical Volume II: Battle Summaries. Washington, D.C.:National Park Service, 1997 Internet Edition. <http://www2.cr.nps.gov/abpp/battles/ok004.htm>. Accessed 28 Sept. 1999.

9 Scott, Preacher 212.

10 Official Records (OR). The Civil War CD-ROM: The War of the Rebellion: A Compilation of the Official Records of the Union and Confederate Armies. Version 1.5 CD-ROM. Carmel, IN: Guild Press, 1996.Citation: 1-22/1: 52.

11 Scott, Preacher 212.

12 Dyer, Frederick H. A Compendium of the War of the Rebellion Des Moines, IA: Dyer Publishing Co., 1906. Version 1.5 CD-ROM. Carmel, IN: Guild Press, 1996. page 1188.

13 Montgomery, 14.

14 OR 1-22/1: 10.

15 Shea, William L. War in the West: Pea Ridge and Prairie Grove. Boulder, CO: Ryan Place Publishers, 1996. page 102.

16 OR 1-22/1: 92.

17 OR 1-22/1: 97.

18 OR 1-22/1: 92.

19 OR 1-22/1: 98.

20 Scott, Preacher 214.

21 Scott, Preacher 215.

22 Dyer, 1188.

23 "Veterans Record of Colonel Thomas Ewing." National Archives and Records Administration, Washington, D.C.: Weer letter 10 Jan. 1863.

24 Burke, 332.

25 Ibid.

26 Senator James H. Lane to President Abraham Lincoln, 13 Mar 1863. Available at Abraham Lincoln Papers at the Library of Congress, Manuscript Division Washington, D.C.: American Memory Project, 2000-01. Internet Address: http://memory.loc.gov/ammem/alhtml/malhome.html

27 Hirshson, Stanley P. The White Tecumseh. New York, NY: John Wiley & Sons, Inc., 1997. pages 85-86, 128-129, 244; Ron Smith Unpublished Research E-Mail to author 12 Mar 2001 [Story of Thomas Ewing III, 26 Feb 1896 found by Smith in the Thomas Ewing Collection, Library of Congress, box 214].

28 Veterans Record of Colonel Thomas Ewing, Order 26 Apr. 1863.

CHAPTER VI

POLICING THE BORDER

Everybody, almost the entire population of
Jackson County and Vernon and Cass and
Bates counties, all of them were depopulated,
and the people had to stay in posts. They called
them posts, but what they were, they were
concentration camps...Then the Federal soldiers
came in and took everything that was left and
set fire to the houses...

Harry S. Truman

    If General Thomas Ewing had not made political enemies prior to assuming command of the Border District (a military district containing the first tier of counties along each side of the Kansas-Missouri line), many would have considered him the devil by the time he left. Ewing's assignment amounted to keeping the peace and being a police officer in an area boiling with hatreds. Previous commanders to the area had been reassigned routinely. The job was an impossible task when Ewing assumed command, as no one commander could satisfy both Kansans and Missourians. During his tenure on the Border, four major events occurred: martial law in Leavenworth, the collapse of a prison, the Lawrence Massacre, and the imposition of General Order Number 11. Two of these would follow him for the rest of his life.

    On June 9, 1863, General John Schofield, commander of the district of Missouri, issued General Order Number 48.

The order redefined the military district boundaries in the Department of Missouri. In part, the order stated: "...Kansas north of the 38th parallel, and the two western tiers of counties of Missouri north of the same parallel and south of the Missouri River will constitute the District of the Border."[1]

On June 16, 1863, Ewing arrived with the impossible order to protect the good citizens of Kansas and to root out bushwhackers (Confederate guerrilla fighters often glamorized as partisan rangers). After arriving in Kansas City, General Ewing established his headquarters at the Pacific House Hotel, 401 Delaware Street, on the southeast corner of Delaware and Fourth Streets (figure 5). The three story, L-shaped structure had a corbeled brick cornice and cast iron arcade. The Pacific House's mortar was barely dry in 1861 when Major General Samuel Sturgis commandeered it for a Union barracks. Before Ewing took it over as his headquarters, the Union barracks also doubled as a hospital.[2] However, Ewing was not destined to sit out his command behind a desk at the hotel.

The next day, fourteen Union soldiers were ambushed and killed near Westport, Missouri. Within days, Ewing's troops tracked down many of the bushwhackers and the Kansas newspapers were singing Ewing's praises. One week after taking command, Ewing spoke to the townspeople of Olathe, Kansas. The General stated that he hoped to have enough troops to prevent raids into Kansas and to sweep out or kill all the guerrillas. He continued by saying he would keep one thousand men in pursuit of the rebels and "redden" every road with their blood.[3] By no means did Ewing plan a one-sided war against Missourians; he intended as well to combat Red Legs and Jayhawkers.

Figure 5. The Pacific House Hotel, 401 Delaware Street, Kansas City, MO. Built in 1861, the hotel was immediately taken over by the Union Army, as it was the only three story building in the city at that time. From here, General Order Number 11 was issued.

The hotel stands to this day and has been largely restored, except for a canopied entrance which is on the left of the picture. Source: Negative # V-894. Special Collections, Kansas City Public Library, Kansas City, MO. Used with permission.

C. M. Chase provided this differentiation between the two terms:

> A *Jayhawker* is a Unionist who professes to rob, burn out and murder only rebels in arms against the government. A *Red Leg* is a Jayhawker originally distinguished by the uniform of red leggings [often worn by members of the Kansas State Militia]. A Red Leg, however, is regarded as more purely an indiscriminate thief and murderer than the Jayhawker... [4]

Colonel Charles R. Jennison was the most infamous Red Leg and regularly entered Missouri to burn, murder, and pillage. Jennison and others gave the militia and Kansans in general a bad name in Civil War Missouri, and General Ewing had decided to change that. His speech served notice to any who gave "respectability to robbery."[5] To prevent violent interactions between the residents of each state, he established small posts thirteen miles apart along the unprotected Kansas-Missouri border. Ewing thinly spread his soldiers into any troubled spot, regardless of his limited manpower. He tried to keep his word to maintain troops in the saddle, as illustrated by a lament from Colonel Bazel F. Lazear. Lazear had been under Ewing's command in 1863, but by the next year he was writing to his wife complaining of his desk job: "I wish to god we were under General Ewing then I could have some chance of serving with the Regiment."[6] Ewing was an active commander and expected the same of his men. Necessity dictated that his soldiers stay on the move as they were so few in number.

In August, according to General Schofield's records, the Border District had only 106 officers (of which eight were staff officers), 3,073 troops, six pieces of heavy artillery, and fourteen pieces of field artillery.[7] With this small force, Ewing had to organize a detective force, military police, units to combat bushwhackers and to control Red Legs, and had to assign troops to protect his western flank, where Indian relations occasionally were strained. Additionally, Confederate Colonel Shelby and Generals Marmaduke and Price liked to sweep through the area on their raids due to the support of local guerrillas and sympathizers, and also because the terrain consisted of rolling prairie, which was ideal for cavalry. Ewing believed he needed three times the number of federal troops to control the Border, which, at best, was a conservative estimate, considering no hotter border area existed west of Maryland.

General Ewing's first controversial action involved declaring martial law in Leavenworth County, Kansas, on July 19, 1863.[8] The reason Ewing issued the order was due to the interference of Leavenworth's Radical Republican Mayor, Dan R. Anthony, in the efforts of Ewing's detectives to stop black market activities. Periodically, some Kansans raided into Missouri or into other Kansas counties to steal horses, which would be sold in Leavenworth, the largest market place in the state. Anthony, the brother of suffragette Susan B. Anthony, was not involved in horse theft, but, according to Ewing, Anthony also averted his eyes from the illegal activities.[9]

Not only were civilians involved in the black market, but so, too, was Senator Lane. Lane had access to the Leavenworth quartermaster's supplies through his friendship with General Blunt. When Ewing took command, Lane realized his profitable enterprise would collapse, as Ewing would not be his marionette. Lane wrote General Halleck suggesting alternate boundaries for the Border District, but Schofield found out about it and argued against it.[10] The rule of law had to be established in Leavenworth.

Anthony interfered when Ewing's detectives "seized some horses belonging to a colored man, claiming they had been stolen in Missouri" and raised the ire of the new General. Anthony argued that this was a matter of civil law and ordered his police to seize the animals from the military, which they did. General Ewing then declared martial law. Martial law continued in Leavenworth until September 8, when a military guard, acting without Ewing's knowledge, arrested Mayor Anthony without proper charges and took him to Kansas City.[11] Anthony was released twenty-four hours later, after he and other Leavenworth citizens met with General Schofield. The resulting agreement ended martial law in Leavenworth.[12] However, while General Ewing's first controversial actions attempted to control Jayhawker excesses and those of other radical Unionists, his plans did not stop there.

Bushwhackers and Confederate spies, mainly women, traveled freely throughout the area of the Border District and supplied the rebels. In late July, the relatives of several well-known guerrillas were arrested and taken to jail. Among the seventeen or so women taken into custody were three sisters of "Bloody" Bill Anderson and two cousins of Cole Younger. Prior to their arrest:

> These women rode into Kansas City almost daily. They saw everything and talked to those who could give them information that would be of benefit to the guerrillas. They secretly bought pistol-caps and other ammunition...[13]

Unlike the conditions prevalent in nineteenth century jails, the women, by most accounts, received decent treatment. They were allowed to walk the streets of Kansas City during the day under escort. Proper food and medical services were provided regularly. Also, they were not confined to cells. They could socialize, gossip, and knit if they so desired. Although they were living in a prison, the Union soldiers went out of their way to ensure that the women were provided their needs.

When two other holding facilities proved inadequate due to overcrowding and poor sanitation, the army confiscated a row house on the east side of 1425 Grand Avenue, between Twelfth and Thirteenth Streets in Kansas City. The house, built in 1859, was owned by the estate of Robert Thomas, whose son-in-law and beneficiary was the renowned Missouri artist, George Caleb Bingham (figure 6). At the time, Bingham was serving as the Missouri State Treasurer. Bingham enjoyed both painting and politics, often combining both. On more than one occasion, he created an oil painting of some great statesman (for example: Washington, Jefferson, Clay, and General Lyon), then lobbied the state legislature to buy them from him. The Thomas house served as both home and studio to Bingham until 1862, when his family vacated the residence. During his stay, to satisfy his need for a studio, he added a third story to the structure .[14]

The house had been occupied as a prison for two weeks when, on August 14, 1863, the prisoners noticed the second floor ceiling cracking and dust falling. As they attempted to flee, the building fell in on itself. Four of the women died, including one of Anderson's sisters. Another two received injuries, with Anderson's youngest sister suffering crippling ones. Others saved themselves by jumping out of windows and running out onto balconies.[15] General Ewing was immediately blamed and rumors abounded, such as that the girls undermined the building while trying to escape, or Union soldiers rigged the building to collapse. Still others for the next 135 years would characterize the house as dilapidated or as "a rickety structure long abandoned." [16]

The most persistent story suggested that the Union soldiers removed support beams from the building to enlarge the first floor and weakened the structure in doing so. Throughout the rest of his life, Bingham would blame the removal of a beam as the reason for the collapse.

Figure 6. Missouri Artist and Statesman George Caleb Bingham by H. T. Slauther.

Source: Department of Publication of the Missouri Commission, <u>The State of Missouri,</u> Columbia, MO: E. W. Stephens, 1904, page 27.

Lew Larkin, a Bingham apologist, stated that Bingham's building "was not the same structure in which the women perished."[17] Yet, the prison was a three story structure, and Bingham's was the only three story house on the block. Most researchers blame the collapse on the removal of timbers. Recently, Charles F. Harris studied the event. His research discovered that the house was not ramshackle. It was in an upscale area of Kansas City and was only four years old. Apparently, the row house to the south had served as a guardhouse for some time prior to the army's confiscation of the Thomas property. The soldiers remodeled, removing partitions and a center beam of the other house which tied into the wall of the Thomas house, and:

> By the time of the collapse, the center girder running the sixty-foot length of the Cockrell building had sagged, and the joists resting thereon tipped at the center of the building. This created a lever action on the common wall between the two buildings. This torquing action caused the Thomas building to fall top over into the Cockrell building. Once the wall began to tilt, the weight of the third story added to the Thomas building by Bingham probably contributed to the collapse. [18]

This accident caused Bingham's disdain of General Ewing, which led to his future personal attacks.[19] Was Ewing or anyone to blame? Ewing most likely knew little more than that a house had been taken over and used as a prison. The soldiers, who removed the Cockrell house beam, performed their actions unthinkingly, without malice. So, if Ewing or Ewing's men were not to blame, was anyone? To think of it as an accident that was caused by a removed timber, which was accelerated by the added weight of a third floor, was to place some unintentional blame on Bingham.[20] The artist could not accept that line of thought. For, if he was partially responsible for the death of those women, was he also partially liable for helping to touch off the Lawrence Massacre? Mentally, he could not accept that it was an accident due to construction and blamed Ewing instead. Still, this event, at least in the eyes of bushwhackers who wished revenge, was no accident. The entire incident played into the hands of one guerrilla, William Quantrill.

William Quantrill conceived the next major event of Ewing's service on the Border long before 1863. Ever since Jim Lane raided and destroyed Osceola, the thought of raiding Lawrence had been in the partisan captain's mind, but he could never quite persuade enough men to ride with him.[21] In 1863, the Border command took increasingly aggressive actions against rebel sympathizers. As the stakes rose, more and more guerrillas leaned toward Quantrill's point of view. Then, General Ewing took command and seemed to have a plan of action. Increased patrols. Forts on the border. Garrisoned towns. The noose had tightened. A rumor that Union soldiers would depopulate the counties by driving out rebel sympathizers persisted.[22] By July 1863, Ewing's spies, who had infiltrated some guerrilla bands, reported that Quantrill would sack Lawrence during the full moon. July's full moon waxed and waned without Quantrill appearing. A collective sigh of relief was heard. On August 14, the prison collapsed. Four days later, General Ewing notified Confederate sympathizers in the Border District that they were to leave by issuing General Order Number 10 (see appendix A for the entire text). General Ewing had raised the stakes again.

Previously, General Ewing established small military posts along the border and directed that some towns, including Lawrence, be garrisoned. The 11th Kansas, under the command of Major Edmund Ross, patrolled the Lawrence area.[23] When the July scare loomed, Lawrence received additional troops. As the fear subsided, only fifteen troops remained camped near Lawrence, across the Kansas River, which logistically presented a problem as any movement into town required the use of a ferry.[24]   After one of his spies reported the Federal troop movements to him, Quantrill readied his gang for action.[25]

On August 21, 1863, Quantrill attacked. Before leaving Lawrence, over one hundred and fifty men were killed and over two hundred buildings destroyed at an estimated cost of $2.5 million.[26] When word reached Major Plumb in Kansas City, he organized a pursuit. Likewise, General Ewing hurried from Leavenworth. Although Ewing's forces caught and killed a few guerrillas, the majority escaped.   The people of Kansas demanded blood.   Some demanded Ewing's.   What was he doing in Leavenworth? Was Ewing at fault? What could be done?

The most embarrassing problems for General Ewing concerned his whereabouts at the time of the massacre and his response to the threat. In the same August 25 report to General Schofield which informed him of General Order Number 11, General Ewing reported:

> I left my headquarters to go to
> Leavenworth the day before the massacre,
> on public business. I have never taken an
> hour of ease or rest with anything undone
> which I thought necessary for the
> protection of the border. [27]

Can an inference be made that his business was not military in nature?   To a degree, yes.   Martial law in Leavenworth was still going on at the time.   While Dan Anthony provided a military purpose for him to go to that city, he easily could have either stopped by a LP&W director's office and asked if anything important was going on, or visited friends.   So, although his duties would require him to periodically inspect his policing efforts in the black market town of Leavenworth, his absence from Kansas City at that crucial time proved a major embarrassment. The radical press questioned the visit to his Kansas home town and Ewing never provided them with an answer.

In the above report to Schofield, Ewing decried the newspapers and Radicals who disliked his martial law order as those who "wish me for a burnt-offering to satisfy the just passion of the people."[28] Additionally, he asked that a military court of inquiry be convened, at General Schofield's discretion, to determine if he was at fault. His words described both his exasperation and his chagrin.

The implication that he was not at his post embarrassed him, and his response to the raid clearly showed how greatly it rattled his nerves. Upon learning of the raid, he saddled up and rode through the dusty prairie in the hot August sun with any soldiers he could gather. When they reached the Kansas River, they had to wait five hours to ferry across. Driving on, without rest, Ewing's column suffered. Horses died and men suffered heat exhaustion, including "Lieutenant Dick, who accompanied me, and who fell dead on dismounting to rest."[29] Some contemporaries suggested at the time that it would have been better had he boarded a riverboat with the troops and horses, traveled to Kansas City and disembarked with fresh troops.[30] The General, who Benjamin F. Simpson described as having the most tremendous mind ever to be in Kansas, definitely failed to make use of it on that day.[31] That was his greatest embarrassment.

On August 25, 1863, Ewing issued General Order Number 11, which Kansas Governor Charles Robinson would lament as the "most humiliating confession of the utter failure of the war of rapine permitted, if not encouraged, by officials..."[32] The order directed all residents of the Missouri counties of Jackson, Cass, Bates and the northern quarter of Vernon County, who did not live within one mile of Harrisonville, Kansas City, Independence, Hickman's Mill or Pleasant Hill, to leave the counties within fifteen days (see Appendix A for the entire order). If loyalty could be proven, then the order allowed people to move within one mile of one of the above named towns.[33] Ewing saw this as a means to clear the area of bushwhackers and have peace in the Border

District once and for all. For, "I intend to destroy the houses of all persons in the border counties, outside of military stations, who do not remove, in obedience to my last general order, by the 9th day of September next."[34]

He also saw this as a way to prevent Senator Lane and other Kansans from going across the border and committing their own massacre. Senator Lane constantly threatened such actions in his public speeches. During the Lawrence massacre, the guerrillas almost caught him in his sleeping gown, but he fled before their arrival and hid in a cornfield the entire time his house burned. After Quantrill's men left, he spent the rest of the day organizing a posse and pursuing them. He continued into the next day.[35]

On the night of the twenty-second, he met General Ewing at Morristown, Missouri. At this point, the story becomes third-hand hearsay. According to the statement of Lieutenant William Mowdry of "some Kansas militia" as reported to Colonel E. F. Rogers "of one of the Missouri regiments" who relayed it to William Connelley, "Ewing begged hard for his official head." Lane told him that he would not complain about Ewing if he issued the order to depopulate the counties. They then entered a cabin and put the finishing touches on the order that Ewing and Schofield had been discussing for the past month. When they came out, Lane said: "You are a dead dog if you fail to issue that order as agreed between us." [36] Ewing was not one to beg. Most likely, Ewing's ingratiating manner and attempts to calm the hot-headed Senator were misunderstood by the soldier. Still, the events of the day had the General clearly shaken.

Upon learning about the massacre, and unaware that General Ewing had already issued the order, General Schofield wrote Ewing:

> I inclose [sic] a draught of an order which
> I propose to issue in due time...But it
> occurs to me as at least probable that the
> massacre and burning at Lawrence was the

immediate consequence of the inauguration of the policy of removing from the border counties the slaves of rebels and the families of bushwhackers [Order Number 10]. If this is true, it would seem a strong argument against the wisdom of such policy... I am pretty much convinced that the mode of carrying on the war on the border during the past two years has produced such a state of feeling that nothing short of total devastation of the districts which are made the haunts of guerrillas will be sufficient to put a stop to the evil... [37]

Both Ewing and Schofield were thinking along the same lines. However, Schofield desired much harsher action. While Ewing only wanted to destroy the houses of those who failed to move, Schofield wanted all disloyal persons removed from the area and then every house, barn, grain, or other property burned. Anything the troops could use that the refugees left behind could be seized. He also did not provide for differentiating loyal from disloyal citizens. However, by September 8, Schofield had a change of heart and directed Ewing that property be protected and that only the property of disloyal citizens would be confiscated for use by the soldiers.[38] Yet, by that date, many homesteads that had been vacated early were most likely already destroyed. Order Number 11 could have been worse. John Speer, a Lane supporter, considered it the harshest act of the war "administered by a just man."[39] John Edwards, General JO Shelby's adjutant and author of Noted Guerrillas, certainly thought it could have been worse, and commented that it was "mercifully" executed.[40] But was it necessary?

That fall, Bingham traveled to Kansas City to recover damages for his three story collapsed house. Although later stories fictionalized the meeting between Ewing and Bingham by emphasizing that Bingham allegedly threatened to make the General "infamous with pen and brush as far as I am able," the collapsed prison was definitely part of the conversation.[41] According to Bingham's December 21, 1863, letter to James S. Rollins, Ewing "would only Certify that the building was thus occupied..." The artist explained in the past tense that he presented facts to the General. He wrote: "Had I been a Kansas horse thief he would have certified to all the facts, proof of which I laid before him..." [42] His letter failed to mention anything about a discussion over the controversial order. He spoke only of his personal damages. Bingham's own words told the truth. If he had been outraged by the Order, would he not have written about a heated discussion with Ewing to his best friend?

Apparently, Bingham, or another family member, liked to embellish bedtime stories for children. Another story has the artist riding on a train with Red Leg Colonel Jennison. In that story, Bingham "made such a violent verbal assault on him that he [Jennison] was glad to escape at the first opportunity." [43] No rational person would verbally attack a man alleged to have committed many murders upon first meeting him. Both stories are deliberately designed to place the artist in a glowing light. Curtis Rollins admitted the Jennison incident was a story, but "I have no doubt of its truth."[44]

Besides using Rollins as a source, Lew Larkin stated that his source was the artist's granddaughter, Clara King Bowdry, of Fort Worth, Texas, who, although not present at the meeting, added "many details, especially in reconstructing the conversation."[45] So, while Bingham may have spoken to General Ewing concerning Order Number 11, the conversation was reconstructed by others. Therefore, the idea of the artist-statesman going forth like "a knight in shining armor" was fanciful and belied his true purpose: to demand compensation for his house.[46] Regardless of the legend's truth, George Caleb Bingham certainly did not think the order was necessary and, at

Figure 7. "Order No. 11" or "Martial Law." Originally copyrighted as: "Civil War: as realized in the Desolation of Border Counties of Missouri during the operation of 'General Order No. 11,' issued by Brigadier General Ewing, from his Head Quarters, Kansas City, August 25, 1863." Ewing is represented on horseback above the white bearded Southern patriarch. Source: Library of Congress, Prints & Photographs Division, Reproduction # LC-USZ62-808.

some point, decided to immortalize the drama in oil. While the Missouri artist never believed Order Number 11 was a proper military directive, five reasons validate the issuance of General Order Number 11. First of all, a military need existed to deprive bushwhackers of their support. Secondly, Kansans needed to feel secure after Lawrence. Third, Ewing needed to suppress the mob violence that Lane was advocating. Fourth, he needed to counter the accusations of his adversaries. Finally, Ewing needed to pacify Lane to remain in his political good graces. [47] One other reason which ties into the first is military action.

General Ewing had considered for some time issuing this directive, and, after doing so, he also had planned to force a military resolution upon the guerrillas.

The Order dictated that all residents were required to leave by September 9. After that date, military operations were to begin. The idea was to push from the north in Jackson County and to move toward waiting Union troops in the southern part of the affected area in the hope of trapping the guerrillas. When operations started, soldiers assisted people who refused to leave. By October, with Ewing actively enforcing the Order and conducting a military action aimed at weeding out bushwhackers, and with the approaching winter, the guerrillas moved south. However, instead of entering the trap, they slipped into Kansas. As they neared Baxter Springs on October 6, they attacked a group of Union soldiers at a small fort. Then, unexpectedly, a Union column appeared in the distance. The soldiers did not hear the fighting, and the guerrillas turned on them. The column was commanded by a surprised General James Blunt. The guerrillas killed seventy of his one hundred men and Blunt only escaped because he had a swift horse.[48] It was the last large scale guerrilla attack on Kansas soil.

Prior to the Baxter Springs incident, the military operations Ewing planned had not been entirely implemented before they ground to an unexpected halt. Colonel JO Shelby had crossed into Missouri from Arkansas on September 30 at the head of six hundred cavalrymen .[49] For the next several weeks, General Ewing's units had to stop their search for guerrillas and coordinate with Generals Egbert Brown and Odin Guitar in central Missouri. Brown and Ewing failed to communicate on a regular basis, causing the latter concern on more than one occasion.[50] The lack of communications proved to be one of the saving graces for Shelby, who escaped Brown's troops at Boonville, charged through a deadly trap set by Colonel Lazear at Marshall, and was chased by Ewing along his avenue of retreat. In the early morning hours of October 18, Ewing caught up with him at Carthage, Missouri.

The night before Ewing's arrival, Shelby's units bivouacked in and around the town. Shelby, with his main force, set up camp at the Kenrick Farm to the north of the Jasper county seat.[51] Major Pickler commanded the troops in the town proper and failed to post sentries. At daylight, Shelby awoke to cannon fire from the town as Pickler's men were caught by surprise.[52]

Upon hearing the opening fire, Shelby sent five companies to fight a delaying action while the main body escaped. His skirmishers checked the Union advance for one hour, giving the crafty Colonel time to escape. Ewing captured Major Pickler and only thirty men. Locally, this brief affair is known as the Second Battle of Carthage.[53]

Because of Shelby, Ewing's planned sweep through the area was only partially successful. The Baxter Springs Massacre is proof of the partial failure, but Ewing cannot be entirely blamed for that. Prior to October, his operations were having some success. Writing home on September 27, Colonel Lazear informed his wife that, "Since I came from home we [referring only to his regiment] have killed and wounded at least fifty guerrilla and captured nearly one hundred horses."[54] Except for the aberration of Baxter Springs, if the goal was to keep guerrilla activity away from Kansas, then it was completely successful since guerrilla activities moved into central Missouri and out of the Border District.

96

Other factors played a part in the reduction of guerrilla activity the following year. First, Quantrill and his captains began to quarrel more. Then Quantrill suffered loss of face with many of his men when George Todd threatened him and the guerrilla leader backed down.[55] Second, the sadistic "Bloody Bill" Anderson died shortly after his massacre at Centralia, Missouri in 1864. Third, the loss of one guerrilla leader and the loss of face for another created divided loyalties, causing the bands to split into smaller units. Groups of one hundred or less men could not commit carnage on the scale of Lawrence. Fourth, military forces were bolstered in both states. All of these circumstances combined with Ewing's actions, so that the military picture of 1864 was markedly different from the situation at the time Ewing assumed command of the Border.

By November 20, 1863, the Border was sufficiently quiet that General Ewing was able to issue Order Number 20, partially rescinding Order 11. The next year, General Brown (Ewing's replacement in the border area) issued another Order Number 11 and fully rescinded it. Not surprisingly, after Brown issued his order, the populace returned and bushwhacking activities increased.[56]

What effects did Ewing's General Order Number 11 have on the populace and the area? The land was devastated, and the nickname "The Burnt District" was given to the area. The name stuck for years to come. Regardless, Lane, Jennison, and others had destroyed many homes before the Order's issuance. The name given to the chimneys without attached buildings was Jennison's Monuments, not Ewing's Monuments. General Ewing knew better than to use Jennison or Lane during the Order's execution. Part of his reasoning for issuing the order was to prevent uncontrolled retaliation by Kansans. The Order achieved that purpose.[57] Additionally, Schofield had expressly forbade Ewing the use of Kansas militia units in Missouri. Rather than use militia, he used troops from other states. He also trusted and used his 11th Kansas, which was a

97

US volunteer regiment and, as such, not part of the state militia.

As to the number of people driven off their lands, that figure is a matter of extreme speculation. Most historians validate the figure of 20,000 refugees, but a minority suggest the number 10,000. Some of the refugees claimed as many as 100,000, which is a highly suspicious number considering that less than 45,000 people populated the area in the 1860 census.[58] The most difficult numbers to reconcile would be the numbers who left their homes for the protection of Kansas or a nearby fort prior to the Order being issued. On June 18, 1863, the sheriff and the county clerk of Cass County wrote General Ewing the following:

> Many of the citizens of this county have moved to and near this post [Harrisonville] for protection, and are endeavoring to support their families by farming around and near the post. Their families and all their effects are here. All the county records and papers are here, and it would be an irreparable loss to the county if we should lose our records. The citizens have had to leave their crops to assist in protecting the post; and, as the time is short for working their crops, if they are not soon relieved they will lose the same.[59]

On June 30, General Ewing reported the following to Lieutenant Colonel Marsh, the Assistant Adjutant General of the Department of Missouri:

> Captain Coleman reports to me that nearly all the Union families in the town [Butler] left there some days before he was ordered away with a militia company which went to Germantown, Henry County, and the rest of the Union families came with him to Kansas. He says there are no Union

98

families in the county, and all the
secessionists known to have been in the
Southern army from that county are again
at home or in the brush...[60]

The General, in the same letter, communicated that
guerrillas had burnt the town of Butler, in Bates County, on
June 21. To General Ewing, the obvious conclusion to such
reports was that few loyal people remained in the area and, of
those people, probably two-thirds actively supported the
guerrillas.[61] Both rebel sympathizers and Yankee soldiers
estimated that eighty percent supported the bushwhackers by
sympathy, but the other twenty percent supported them due to
fear.[62]

General Ewing's estimate of two or three hundred
refugee families affected by Order No. 11 is a low number.[63]
However, a population projection, based on the statements
made concerning the effects of the war on another border
county, lends credulity to the count of 10,000 people (See
Appendix B).

To this day, apologists for Missouri guerrillas write
diatribes calling this the most horrific abuse of military power
against United States citizens. Some denounce throwing people
out of their homes in the winter (September 9 is still warm in
Missouri), while others, such as President Truman, call the
posts concentration camps. Can we say that this was worse than
Sheridan's push through the Shenandoah Valley? Or the
burning of Atlanta? What of the Mormon extermination order?
Or the massacre at Wounded Knee? Not to mention
Roosevelt's Japanese relocation order. In modern terms, think
of the British carpet bombing of German cities or the dropping
of an atomic bomb. What is more merciful: simply dropping
the bombs or warning people before the bombs fall? Would it
have been better for a family to be awakened by a cannon ball
crashing through the side of the house? The order was, to a
degree, a show of mercy.

When citizenry actively supports the enemy, they are

subject to the laws of war. When the Confederate States justified supporting and endorsing the use of guerrillas (partisan rangers) as a military necessity, which they did when they commissioned William Quantrill as a captain, then they forced the citizenry to provide the guerrillas sustenance. Citizens became combatants and targets under the laws of war because the actions of the guerrillas were endorsed by the rebel command. The actions of the Confederate government justified the Union expulsion of citizens under General Order Number 11. The purpose of Ewing's Orders Numbers Ten and Eleven was "not to undermine the Confederacy's political and economic ability to resist, but rather to curb civilians so that the conventional military contest could proceed."[64]

1 Official Records [OR]. The Civil War CD-ROM: The War of the Rebellion: A Compilation of the Official Records of the Union and Confederate Armies. Version 1.5 CD-ROM. Carmel, IN: Guild Press, 1996.Citation: 1-22/2: 315.

2 Cantrell, Scott. "A Legend Aloft: Pacific House to be back among the living in River Market." Kansas City Star 26 July 1998. Internet Library Search, page 1-2.

3 Goodrich, Thomas. Bloody Dawn: The Story of the Lawrence Massacre. Kent,
OH: Kent State University Press, 1991. page 21.

4 Ibid, 21.

5 Castel, Albert. Civil War Kansas: Reaping the Whirlwind. Lawrence, KS: University Press of Kansas, 1997. page 112.

6 McLarty, Vivian Kirkpatrick, ed. "The Civil War Letters of Colonel Bazel F. Lazear." Mssouri Historical Review Vol. 92 No 4 (1998): 393-406. Columbia, MO: State Historical Society of Missouri. page 405.

7 OR 1-22/2: 504.

8 OR 1-22/2: 388.

9 OR 1-22/2: 389.

10 Castel, Albert. Civil War Kansas: Reaping the Whirlwind, 111.

11 Cutler, William G. "History of the State of Kansas: Leavenworth County, Kansas Collection Books." Internet Edition. Topeka, KS: Kansas State Historical Society, n.d.

12 Schofield, John M. Forty-Six Years in the Army. Norman, OK: University of Oklahoma Press, 1998. page 84; Cutler, Leavenworth.

13 Connelley, William Elsey. Quantrill & The Border Wars. New York, NY: Smithmark, 1996. page 299.

14 Harris, Charles F. "Catalyst for Terror: The Collapse of the Women's Prison in Kansas City." Missouri Historical Review Vol. 89 No. 2 (1995): 290-306. Columbia, MO: The State Historical Society of Missouri. page 295.

15 Ibid, 300.

16 Johnson, Clint. Civil War Blunders. Winston-Salem, North Carolina: John F. Blair, Publisher, 1997. page 259; Larkin, Lew. Bingham: Fighting Artist. Point Lookout, MO: School of the Ozarks Press, 1971. page 153.

17 Larkin, 227.

18 Harris, Catalyst 302.

19 Rash, Nancy. The Paintings & Politics of George Caleb Bingham, New Haven, CT: Yale University Press, 1991.page 191.   20 Confederate Military History Vol 1-12 CD-ROM. Carmel, IN: Guild Press,

1997. Citation Vol. 9, 188.

21 Harris, "Letter to author," 5 Oct. 1999.

22 Niepman, Ann Davis. "General Order No. 11 and Border Warfare During the Civil War." Missouri Historical Review Vol. 66 No 2 (1972): 185-210. Columbia, MO: State Historical Society of Missouri. page 198.

23 OR 1-22/2: 762.

24 Schultz, Duane. Quantrill's War. New York, NY: St. Martin's Press, 1996. page 152.

25 Ibid144.

26 Goodrich, Thomas. Black Flag: Guerrilla Warfare on the Western Border, 1861-1865. Bloomington, IN: Indiana University Press, 1995. page 94.

27 OR 1-22/2: 473.

28 Ibid.

29 OR 1-22/2: 582-583.

30 Goodrich, Bloody 152.

31 Simpson, Benjamin F. "The Wyandotte Constitution." Kansas Historical Collections 2 (1875-1880): 236-247. Topeka, KS: KSHS. page 243.

32 Robinson, Charles. Kansas Conflict. Freeport, NY: Books for Libraries Press, 1972. page 448.

33 OR 1-22/2: 473.

34 OR 1-22/2: 480.

35 Speer, John. Life of Gen. James H. Lane, "The Liberator of Kansas." Garden City, KS: John Speer Printer 1896. page 267; Connelley, 352.

36 Connelly, 417; Schultz, 140.

37 OR 1-22/2: 471.

38 Schofield, 84.

39 Speer, 332.

40 Edwards, John N. Noted Guerrillas. St. Louis, MO: Bryan, Brand and Co., 1877. page 206.

41 Rollins, C. B., ed. "Letters of George Caleb Bingham to James S. Rollins, Part V." Missouri Historical Review Vol. 33 No. 1 (1938): 45-78. Columbia, MO: State Historical Society of Missouri. page 65.

42 Ibid, 62.

43 Ibid, 46.

44 Rollins 46

45 Larkin, 344.

46 Ibid, 195.

47 Castel, Albert. Civil War Kansas: Reaping the Whirlwind, page 142-144.

48 Monaghan, Jay. <u>Civil War on the Western Border: 1854-1865</u>. Lincoln, NE: First Bison Books, 1984. page 294.

49 OR 1-22/1: 671.

50 OR 1-22/1: 662.

51 Cottrell, 33.

52 OR 1- 22/1: 663.

53 Cottrell, 34.

54 McLarty, 398.

55 Connelley, 450.

56 Castel, Albert. "Order No. 11 And The Civil War On The Border." <u>Missouri Historical Review</u> Vol. 57, No. 4 (1963): 357-368. Columbia, MO: The State Historical Society of Missouri. page 367.

57 Hatley, Paul B. and Noor Ampssler. "Army General Order Number 11: Final Valid Option or Wanton Act of Brutality? The Missouri Question in the American Civil War." <u>Journal of the West Vol</u>. 33 No. 3 (July 1994): 77-87. page 86.

58 Eakin, Joanne Chiles. <u>Tears and Turmoil: Order Number 11</u>. Shawnee Mission, KS: Two Trails Genealogy, 1996. page 103; Kennedy, Joseph C. G. <u>Population of the United States in 1860; Compiled from the Original Returns of the Eighth Census, under the Direction of the Secretary of the Interior</u>. Washington, D.C.: Government Printing Office, 1864. pages 288-291.

59 OR 1-22/2: 325.

60 OR 1-22/2: 376.

61 OR 1-22/2: 428.

62 Castel, Albert. "Order No. 11 And The Civil War On The Border." page 366.

63 "Ewing Speaks." <u>Kansas City Daily Times</u>. 7 Aug. 1879..

64 Grimsley, Mark. The Hard Hand of War: Union Military Policy Toward Southern <u>Civilians 1861-1865</u>. New York, NY: Press Syndicate of the University of Cambridge, 1995. page 119.

CHAPTER VII

THE BATTLE OF PILOT KNOB

"... this is the hottest battle I was ever in."
Captain William J. Campbell. 14th Iowa
27 Sep. 1864

Two major studies exist concerning the Battle of Pilot Knob: Cyrus Peterson and Joseph Hanson's Pilot Knob: Thermopylae of the West and Brice Suderow's Thunder In The Arcadia Valley. Both cover in detail the battle and its aftermath. The Pyrrhic victory for General Sterling Price's Confederate forces proved so costly that Price could not move against Saint Louis or Jefferson City. This reduced Price's campaign to field maneuvers and ultimately led to his defeat at Westport. General Ewing felt that he never received the acclaim that he deserved for this victory. What should he have expected in a backwater area of the Civil War? The Union already controlled the Mississippi and what were seen as more decisive battles were being fought in the East. Still, it was a great battle, a great victory, famous in the nineteenth century. Indeed, the battle remained famous past the turn of the century, as exemplified by Buffalo Bill Cody's biography. Written in 1899 by his sister, the account detailed Cody's actions as a Union spy during the battle (although no known independent source verifies this story or his presence).[1]

On February 28, 1864, General Ewing almost disappeared from the pages of history. The army reassigned him to the Department of Kansas, Fifth District of Colorado, as its commander. Nonetheless, he never assumed that post. By

March 16, he was working for the newly-appointed commander of the District of Missouri, General William Rosecrans. Whether Ewing or Rosecrans manipulated this move remains a matter of speculation. Anti-Ewing writers consistently suggest that Ewing needed out of Kansas because of public outrage due to Order Number 11. However, several months had passed since he had issued the order. Fall and winter slipped by quietly, as the guerrilla activity had been curbed, which allowed the General to partially rescind the order. Therefore, public outrage is not the entire answer. In all likelihood, his transfer was due to an ongoing process of restructuring command and to Rosecrans requesting the beleaguered General, as he wished for Ewing to sell Sherman on a plan. Rosecrans wanted to combine all troops west of the Mississippi under his command "to sweep the country...clear to the Gulf, including Texas ultimately."[2] One possible reason for Rosecrans's request was that he had worked with the Ewings before and trusted them. Hugh Ewing had previously served as one of his staff officers. Whatever the chief reason may be for the transfer, Brigadier General Thomas Ewing became the commander of the District of Saint Louis, with his first assignment being a meeting with Sherman.

Sherman telegraphed Ewing to meet him at Pana, Illinois, on March 18. Ewing arrived at Pana and met both Sherman and General Ulysses S. Grant. The three traveled eastbound in a private rail car, during which time Sherman outlined his plan for a march through Georgia ending at the sea. However, at this first presentation of the idea, Grant approved the march only as far as Atlanta. After Grant left them, Ewing and Sherman traveled back to Pana. During their private time together, Ewing asked Sherman why he was accompanying the generals. Sherman replied that he wanted a man he could trust as a witness to his conversations with Grant. It was at this time that Sherman asked Ewing to accompany him on the march and said that he would make him a major-general. Ewing kept his reasons for declining private from everyone; however, a likely hypothesis would be that he wanted to be closer to his business interests and the politics of Kansas should the chance to be Senator arise. During the time the two brothers-in-law conversed, Sherman read Rosecrans's dispatch. On March 19, Sherman wrote his response declining to put Rosecrans in charge of all operations west of the Mississippi.[3]

Upon General Ewing's return to Saint Louis, he woke his adjutant and told him of Sherman's offer and that he did not accept it. Adjutant Harrison Hannahs told him, "General, you have made the mistake of your life!" Ewing went home and woke his wife, who uttered the same words.[4] Could his attempts to stay close to his business and political interests ultimately have hurt his long-term chances at a political office?

General Ewing's duties in eastern Missouri were similar to those on the west side, with one exception; the Mississippi provided a good barrier between free and slave states. Additionally, with most of the guerrilla skirmishes concentrated in southern Missouri, the General was able to concentrate his forces in that region. Despite the river's protection and the limited guerrilla threat, the General acted as aggressively against bushwhackers and their sympathizers as he had on the Border. Would he have done so if he viewed Order Number 11 as a mistake? While rebels and copperheads decried the order, true Unionists generally applauded it, as evidenced by the fact that some people on the western border actively sought his return. On June 4, 1864, C. Carpenter of Kansas City petitioned General Rosecrans:

> *The Union men generally are dissatisfied with General Brown's course toward rebel sympathizers in this section of country...The policy of General Brown gives Union men no protection. The people, the loyal Union men, are desirous of a change of commanders in this department or district. They are desirous, and wish, that General Ewing may be sent in the place of General Brown. General Ewing has the*

confidence of the people; they look upon him as
the only man that understands the situation of
this district of country.[5]

However, Ewing was to stay in eastern Missouri, responsible for a district stretching into southeastern Missouri, southern Illinois, and western Kentucky. As the new military commander, his actions in eastern Missouri bore a resemblance to those harsh measures he had taken in the west. On June 7, 1864, General Ewing issued a directive to the commanding officer at Cape Girardeau, Missouri:

> You will keep your men in the saddle as constantly as possible to destroy the small band of guerrillas who are swarming all around you, killing and robbing. Instruct Captain Ewing [unrelated] and all your subordinates that these rebels are not to be captured under any circumstances, but to be killed when found. If a man is not known to be a guerrilla and taken without arms, and afterward proves to be a guerrilla, he must be regularly tried. Such trials, however, only result, where the prisoner is convicted, in putting the Government to the expense of boarding and lodging him during the war, as the President rarely approves a sentence of death. It is therefore best to take few prisoners.[6]

Later, after the Battle of Pilot Knob, Ewing ordered Lieutenant Colonel Hiller:

> Southeast Missouri must be renovated or else given up to the rebels. You will adopt a judicious system for driving out of the State the worst sympathizers and the worst families of Confederate soldiers and guerrillas... Where the circumstances are

such that they cannot go this fall without great suffering, let them arrange to go by spring, but in one way or another the worst rebel families in Southeast Missouri must be got out before corn planting. Let me hear what suggestions you have to make, and what steps you take under this order. [7]

Clearly, General Ewing sought a solution in southeastern Missouri similar to the one he had imposed on the Border District. He would not be blamed again for another incident such as Lawrence, Kansas, due to an omission on his part.

During the summer of 1864, every rebel action of any size raised suspicions and gossip that General JO Shelby or General Sterling Price (figure 8) would raid the territory. Since spring, Rosecrans's military intelligence regularly reported that a raid was in preparation.[8] Missourians considered such to be a certainty. A Missouri proverb told that there were five seasons in Civil War Missouri: spring, summer, fall, winter, and Price's Raid.[9] September hosted three seasons that year.

The future of a United States was still in question in 1864. General Sherman had already begun his march to the sea, but large Confederate armies remained intact. The Confederacy needed a plan to take some of the pressure off its eastern armies. Late in July, General Kirby Smith, commander of the Confederacy's Trans-Mississippi Department, received orders to transfer his infantry to Georgia and Alabama. He then advised President Jefferson Davis that he was planning a campaign and Davis rescinded the order. After telling the President a campaign was planned, he then had to devise one.[10] His spies had determined that less than 14,000 Union soldiers were stationed in Missouri.[11] All of Missouri, or at least the storehouses of Saint Louis, might be ripe for picking.

Figure 8   Major-General Sterling Price, former Governor of
Missouri. Source: Carte de visite (circa 1861-1880) in the collection of
the author .

Strategically, the plan might have worked and considerably lengthened the war. What Smith needed to win was a fast moving, Sherman-like general. Instead, he chose Major General Sterling 'Old Pap' Price.

General Price was an ex-Congressman and Governor from Missouri, who had military experience in the Mexican War. In 1861, Price had valiantly and bravely led troops at Wilson's Creek, where he received a wound to his side. At Lexington, Missouri, he defeated the Union soldiers by having his troops use wetted bales of hemp as rolling cover to reach the enemy line. To this day, it is remembered as the Battle of the Hemp Bales. His victory was widely hailed by Missouri secessionists, and, "coming on the heels of Wilson's Creek, it...gave him [Price] an exaggerated opinion of his own military abilities, and led him to underestimate the hazards involved in assaulting fortified positions." [12] With the death of Missouri's Confederate Governor-In- Exile, Claiborne Jackson, early in the war, Old Pap represented the Confederacy to many Missourians.

Price also fought at Iuka and Corinth, Mississippi. He always led his troops on horseback. Brave in battle, he probably would have made an excellent infantry captain. One of Price's great weaknesses was that he routinely failed to see how military strategy could differ from political strategy. Smith's proposed raid into Missouri, Price thought, would cause the people of Missouri to rise up in rebellion against Federal domination, if only a rebel force could maintain a foothold in the state. If he could keep a foothold in Missouri, it might even cost Lincoln his reelection.

As Smith and Price prepared their plans, Price viewed the coming raid to be as much a political campaign for him as a military one for the Confederacy. On September 19, with Generals John Marmaduke, James Fagan, cavalryman JO Shelby and 12,000 soldiers, he moved his command at a slow pace, as if reenacting a Roman triumph, into Missouri, near Doniphan.

Early in the war the Arcadia Valley (figure 9) and nearby Ironton achieved a modicum of fame when Colonel Ulysses S.

Grant received his appointment to Brigadier General there, but September 26 and 27, 1864, became the crowning days in Iron County's history. In the 1820s, the Missouri Iron Company became the first corporation in the state and conducted its business in this iron rich valley. The high quality iron ore became so important in that era of railroad construction, that one of the first railroads in the state operated between Pilot Knob and Saint Louis. When war broke out, the iron supply had to be protected and, for that reason, the Union established (official name) Camp Blood and later built Fort Davidson near the railroad's terminus (figure 10). Fort Davidson was an earthen, hexagonal fort with sloping walls which rose not more than 10 feet above a surrounding dry moat. The fort was the major Union fort between Saint Louis and Little Rock, but Price could have easily skirted it without creating a serious threat to his flank.

On September 24, 1864, using very poor military judgment, General Rosecrans sent General Thomas Ewing south to reinforce the Iron Mountain Railroad, thereby spreading instead of consolidating his troops.[13] On September 26, Ewing learned of Price's movements near Fredericktown and received additional orders to continue down the rail line to Pilot Knob to assess the situation. Rosecrans ordered him to destroy and abandon the fort, railroad, and mine operations, if necessary, but most importantly to determine where Price would strike. This last assignment prevented General Ewing from making a decision on September 26, when his troops first contacted Price's advance scouts.

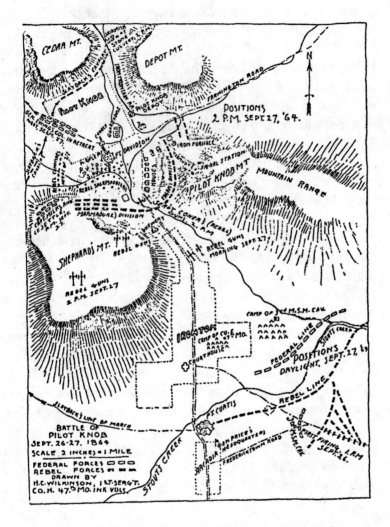

Figure 9. Fort Davidson and Vicinity. Battle Information drawn by Sgt. H.C. Wilkinson, Co. H, 47th MO Infantry. Source: Collection of Jack Mayes.

Figure 10. Fort Davidson, Scaled Model. One
of many displays at Fort Davidson State Historic Site.
Photo by author.

At dusk on September 26, General Ewing still had not seen a major contingent of rebels. Ewing met with his long-time friend, Doctor Seymour Carpenter and the Radical Republican candidate for Missouri governor, Colonel Thomas Fletcher. Fletcher had already served in several battles. On December 29, 1862, he was wounded and captured at Chickasaw Bayou. He was incarcerated at Libby Prison until he was exchanged in May 1863. After that, Fletcher fought at the Battle of Lookout Mountain and served under Sherman in the Atlanta Campaign until he took ill and returned home. In August, 1864, he returned to duty to protect Missouri from Price's reported movements.[14] Now, the General sought Fletcher's and Carpenter's advice on whether to abandon the fort or fight. The Colonel wanted to abandon it. The Doctor appealed to Ewing's desire to be a Senator by advising him that he could not be elected "if they ran away."[15] After leaving them, Ewing met with Adjutant David Murphy, who appealed to the General's sense of honor.[16]

Early in the morning of September 27, 1864, the majority of Price's troops still had not appeared. By 9:00 AM, Confederate forces pushed Ewing's forces back to positions on Pilot Knob Mountain and Shepherd's Mountain, with the gap between them wide open and leading to the fort.

As the main body of Confederate troops approached the gap, Ewing finally knew he was facing a considerable force and that the estimates of 10,000 Butternuts seemed accurate. For a while, the skirmishers repelled the rebels, but more kept arriving. By 11:00 AM, any retreat and demolition of the fort would have been hasty and unsupported by General A. J. Smith to the north. General Shelby's troops had cut telegraph lines and ripped up railroad track along Ewing's most probable avenues of escape. With only 1,262 soldiers and 150 citizens (66 black), General Ewing readied his command for battle.[17]

Confederate troops seized Pilot Knob Mountain and Shepherd's Mountain upon which they placed a cannon. After setting it up, the cannon discharged a few rounds, but Adjutant Murphy accurately estimated the necessary trajectory and returned fire. One shell struck the cannon's wheel and the rebs quickly moved it. Following this event, the future battlefield was relatively quiet for two hours. As Price's forces gathered in the gap, Ewing spent that quiet time before battle dispatching troops to both mountains to keep the rebel forces "in check...as long as possible, before recalling them to the fort."[18]

Around two o'clock in the afternoon, Price attacked. Three separate waves of southern troops assaulted the fort. On the third charge, Confederates reached the moat, but their drive buckled under relentless gunfire and exploding grenades. In just twenty minutes of fighting, over 1,000 rebel soldiers fell.

According to the Daily Missouri Democrat, General Ewing acted cheerful, calm, fearless, heroic, and brave. In a field report that has not been documented elsewhere, the newspaper's correspondent, "Waldo," who watched the battle from the side of Pilot Knob Mountain, recounted:

Several times during the charge General Ewing sallied out of the fort in order to give directions to and encouraging the men in the rifle-pits, exposing himself to the raking fire of the charging rebels. [19]

Sergeant H. C. Wilkinson saw a much different, more august General during the climax of the assault:

I saw the stately form of Gen. Ewing, his arms folded, his mouth tightly closed, and his face slightly pale, but firm as a stone wall. He walked erect from side to side, looking here and there at the surging mass around us. [20]

The result of these attacks were reported by Doctors Carpenter and Thomas Johnson, who claimed "caring for and burying most of the 1,500 casualties."[21] Most present-day historians prefer a count of 1,030 Confederate dead or wounded.[22] General Price's chief engineer reported 1,060 casualties for the assaults on the fort without including casualties over the entire five days of battle.[23] The Daily Missouri Democrat received loss reports on October 3, 1864, and declared:

They probably lost two hundred in killed
and between six and eight hundred wounded

most of them severely. And those who suppose that heavier execution ought to have been done by the small force of a few hundred men under General Ewing, in a few hours, ought to be sent to a lunatic asylum.[24]

The defenders lost considerably fewer men. The Union casualties for the two days evidenced the magnitude of Ewing's victory. There were twelve Union soldiers dead, sixty-five wounded, with 129 men missing, who mostly were "cut off during the confederate [sic] assaults."[25]

General Price decided to storm the fort again the next day. Ewing wanted to stay and fight, but Colonel Fletcher told him that if Ewing stayed, he and his men were leaving.[26] Captain H.B. Milks reported that there was a secret ballot on the decision to fight or evacuate. He further commented, "I voted 'evacuate,' and the result was 'evacuate' by a majority of one."[27] Ewing commanded that the fort be abandoned after midnight. Ewing directed a small squad to sneak into town and clear out rebels. While this order was being carried out, preparations for evacuation began. Muffling the horses' hooves and cannon wheels with sacks and clothing to avoid making noise on the drawbridge, and under cover of darkness, the entire Union army marched out of the fort. They passed within yards of encamped Confederate troops north of the fort, but none challenged them. General Ewing succeeded in escaping to the north in an attempt to meet General Smith at Mineral Point, Missouri (figure 11).

Approximately two, or some say three, in the morning on September 28, 1864, a demolition team left behind by Ewing torched the powder magazine holding about twenty tons of blackpowder. The explosion rocked the valley, and people reportedly heard it twenty miles away. Thinking the blue coats blown up by an accident, Price's troops failed to investigate the explosion until the next morning. Only then did they realize Ewing's forces were intact and only then did Marmaduke begin pursuit. [28]

The morning of the twenty-eighth found Ewing's command near Caledonia, Missouri, about fifteen miles from the Pilot Knob battlefield. At Caledonia, they met an advance guard of Shelby's troops and fought them off. After briefly questioning one rebel prisoner, General Ewing turned his column away from the Potosi Road and headed west to Webster (presently named Palmer).[29] By sunset, they had traveled thirty-one miles from Pilot Knob to Webster, with Shelby and Marmaduke's troops in pursuit. Clinging to the ridge tops, Ewing was able to deny the pursuing rebels an open field to engage in battle and limited the fighting to rear delaying actions. Theodore Russell, one of the Union soldiers picked up the story:

> Instead of following the direct route to Rolla, we took a road that leads over the ridge between the waters of the Courtois and the Huzzah, which leads down into a mountain gorge, through which the Huzzah flows, and thus got on a line of retreat which saved the command from utter destruction. Being upon this mountain ridge, we could not be flanked.[30]

Come nightfall on the twenty-ninth, Ewing was in Leasburg; "having made the march of sixty-six miles in thirty-nine hours."[31] Ewing found a four hundred foot long railroad cut and some railroad ties. He used the ties to barricade the ends of the cuts and to built breastworks on the sides.

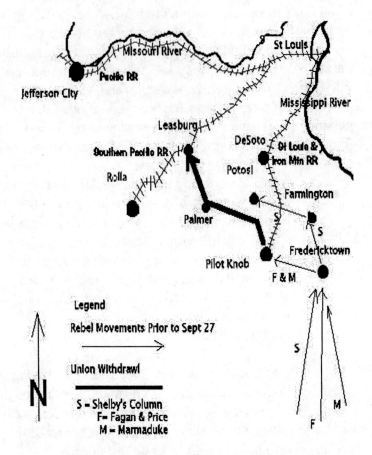

Figure 11. Opening Movements of Price's Raid. Price's army moved out from Pocahontas, Arkansas, about 120 miles due south of Fredericktown. General Shelby took the lead, moving through Fredericktown to attack Farmington and Potosi. This cut Ewing off from his assistance stationed near DeSoto. After an intense battle at Pilot Knob, Ewing successfully disengaged and retreated to Leasburg. Map prepared by author. Source: Peterson & Hanson, Pilot, map supplement.

The rebels tried two more major attacks against Ewing's forces before he could maximize his defenses at Leasburg, but they were driven back. The next day, September 30, the beleaguered Union forces stayed behind the breastworks, exchanging continual fire with the rebels, but no attack came. Marmaduke and Shelby had decided not to attack any more because it could be costly and, in their opinions, because Ewing's force was no longer a factor in the campaign.[32] By that time, Price had wasted five days and he began to recall his scattered troops. At noon on October 1, a 600 man unit from the 17th Illinois reinforced the battle-worn troops. Ewing, however, was still a factor.

Believing correctly that the North now had time to get reinforcements to Saint Louis, General Price decided to forgo attacking Saint Louis and instead advanced toward the capital, Jefferson City.[33] Ewing and his soldiers were finally relieved at Leasburg and sent to Rolla. With these tired soldiers manning Rolla, fresh units from that city moved out to garrison Jefferson City. With Jefferson City reinforced, Price avoided it as well. The pressure was now on, and within a few weeks, Price suffered a strategic defeat at Westport, Missouri, and disaster at Mine Creek, Kansas.

Ewing's decision to hold and fight at Pilot Knob had immediate and direct results. First, the battle cost Price dearly in the number of troops at his disposal, which forced him to by-pass any fortified area like Saint Louis or Jefferson City. Second, Price was also hoping for munitions and other supplies to help his campaign. Instead, he wasted supplies. Third, the carnage demoralized Price's army. Fourth, Price counted on Missourians to rise to his banner, but after such a loss, few sympathizers came forward. Fifth, the chase delayed Price for five days, allowing Saint Louis, which had only 4,500 soldiers garrisoned nearby, to be reinforced with troops who had been enroute to Mobile. Finally, by escaping, Ewing kept the small Union army in Missouri intact, allowing troop transfers to reinforce the capital, Jefferson City. However, Price's Raid succeeded in lengthening the war by as much as four months, and it would have been longer if he had taken a major city. This conclusion is based, in part, on the fact that "[b]y diverting troops from the east, it delayed the Mobile Expedition..." [34] General Thomas Ewing, Jr., standing like King Leonidas at the front of his 300 Spartans at Thermopylae, decided to fight at Fort Davidson in Missouri's Arcadia Valley; that, in a single stroke, prevented lengthening the war beyond that four month period.

Ewing has been criticized for deciding to fight. It was not a militarily sound decision based on the terrain and his orders. Aside from that, some point to one or another errors in his tactics. Ewing needed to use skirmishers to delay the attack, to determine Price's strength, and to limit the rebels to one assault before nightfall on the twenty-seventh. Still, some allege that Ewing went too far. The General sent out one hundred of his best men to the two mountains to harass the enemy. Only fifty men returned to the fort in time for the battle. Supposedly, these fifty were instrumental in repelling Price's assault by defending the drawbridge. Sending them out so near to the time of battle, Ewing could have lost the battle as their skirmishing "no longer served a purpose." [35] The supposition is that if more of Ewing's crack unit had been in the fort, the attack would have been more readily repulsed. Another problem with Ewing's plan was in the use of skirmishers at all, because this "needlessly exposed" them to "life- threatening situations." [36]

Were these men instrumental in saving the fort during the main attacks? According to the story by Captain William J. Campbell, Ewing praised these men as saving "this work." [37] Campbell belonged to the 14th Iowa, and Ewing was dressing-down an officer from another unit who insulted the bravery of the 14th Iowans. That is the gist of Campbell's story. It was Campbell who directed that grenades be tossed into the moat, which prevented the wall from being breached, and ordered men to protect the drawbridge. [38] Campbell was indeed one of the heroes of the day, but the Iowans had arrived with 142 men. [39] Perhaps Ewing was praising the remaining men, or maybe he was speaking of the entire unit's skirmishing abilities. According to Campbell, General Ewing called to him: "Captain, get twenty men,--volunteers,--to stand at the gate till the death!" Campbell replied that he did, but Sergeant H.C. Wilkinson from the 47th Missouri Infantry was the man Campbell secured and the sergeant guarded the gate with only four men.[40] Whatever the meaning of Ewing's cryptic comment, the conclusion cannot be drawn from it that the returning fifty men saved the fort.

Ewing had committed to skirmishing, which was probably the only action that could keep the Confederate troops off-balance. If Ewing had, in the last hours, recalled troops from the mountains, Price and his commanders might have had second thoughts concerning their foolhardy frontal attack. The mountain sides could have been cleared of Union troops and made available for use by rebel cannons. A few well-placed cannon shells would have crippled the defenders, opening the way for a successful attack, but Price and his commanders could not tell if the Union skirmishers in the field were coming from or going to Fort Davidson. The Union skirmishers could have been relief troops arriving to defend the fort. Imagining such a possibility, Price would desire an immediate decision. Since Ewing would not surrender, Price had to attack. Now, as to whether General Ewing should have sent out his best troops, that question ought to be phrased as: "Do I want troops I can trust will not break, panic, or surrender at the first sign of trouble to defend me, or will any troops do?" General Ewing, either by accident or design, made the correct decision.

General Ewing served bravely, actively directing his men during the battle, and received honors from fellow soldiers throughout the rest of his life for his action. Immediately after discovering he had been fooled, General Sterling Price "paid grudging tribute to the defenders, inquiring if Ewing was a West Pointer..."[41] On October 7, at his Saint Louis home on Locust, between Sixth and Seventh Streets, the people of the city gave him a "complimentary serenade."[42] His wife prophesied, "Your career is now onward and upward."[43] The next time President

121

Lincoln saw his father, he would ask, "What do you think of your brat now?"[44] His actions also earned him the brevet to major-general (figure 12) on March 13, 1865. However, he did not receive the triumphant march down the streets of Washington that his foster brother received. On that day in May, 1865, General Ewing merely waited on the reviewing stand to congratulate Sherman the conqueror.

After General Ewing declined General Sherman's offer of command on the March to the Sea, Ellen Ewing said that it was the mistake of Ewing's life. It was not. In the first place, Thomas Ewing, Jr., became a Union General by successfully leading Kansans in two battles and several skirmishes. That was the only background he needed to develop a political life in Kansas, or in any other state after the war. However, assuming that going with Sherman would have helped his political career and that not doing so was his biggest mistake, the casual reader of history must quickly provide the answer to a simple challenge. Name two other generals who were with Sherman on his march through the South! Even the serious student might only name one of his rivals, General Joseph Johnston. Without research, names that include the other two Ewing brothers and McCook are lost in the shadows. The glory belonged to William Tecumseh Sherman. He stood between the sun and any other general in his command. However, the only Union general identified with the Battle at Pilot Knob is Thomas Ewing, Jr. No Union officer there eclipsed him. If there was fault for not receiving acclaim, it was his alone. He could have written an account of his actions as so many other generals did, but he did not. He could have bragged of his exploits during the many speeches he gave throughout his life, but again he did not. Ewing was not the type to brag, although his character would allow him to accept accolades.

Figure 12. Major-General Thomas Ewing, Jr. Source: Photograph No. NWDNS -111-B-4720 (Mathew Brady Studio); "Gen. Thomas Ewing, Jr.;" Office of the Chief Signal Officer; National Archives at College Park, College Park, MD.

1 Wetmore, Helen Cody. Last of the Great Scouts: The Life Story of William F.Cody ("Buffalo Bill" Cody). Electronic text #1248. Project Gutenberg Association: Carnegie-Mellon University, 1998.(Wetmore).

2 Lamers, William M. The Edge of Glory: A Biography of General William S. Rosecrans, U.S.A. New York, NY: Harcourt, Brace & World, 1961. page 419.

3 OR 1-34/2: 656.

4 Hannahs, Harrison. "General Thomas Ewing, Jr." Collections of the Kansas State Historical Society 1911-1912, Vol XII (1912): Topeka, KS: State Printing Office. page 280.

5 OR 1-34/4: 222.

6 OR 1-34/4: 260.

7 OR 1- 41/4: 275.

8 OR 1 Vol. 41/1, 309.

9 Lewis, Lloyd. "Propaganda and the Kansas-Missouri War." Missouri Historical Review 92 No. 2 (1998): 135-148. Columbia, MO: State Historical Society of Missouri. page 136.

10 Brownlee, Richard S. "The Battle of Pilot Knob, Iron County, Missouri, September 26, 1864." Missouri Historical Review Vol. 92, No. 3 (1998): 271-296, Columbia, MO: The State Historical Society of Missouri. page 273.

11 Thompson, Joseph Conan. "The Great-Little Battle of Pilot Knob, Parts 1 and 2." Missouri Historical Review 83 (1989): 139-160,271-294. Columbia, MO: State Historical Society of Missouri. page 140.

12 Castel, Albert. General Sterling Price And the Civil War in the West. Baton Rouge, LA: Louisiana State University Press, 1993. page 56.

13 Brownlee, Richard S. Grey Ghosts of the Confederacy: Guerrilla Warfare in the West 1861-1865. Baton Rouge, LA: Louisiana State University Press, 1984. page 282.

14 Reppy, John H. "Thomas Clement Fletcher." The Messages and Proclamations of the Governors of the State of Missouri, Volume I. Columbia, MO: Missouri State Historical Society, 1922. <gopher://mosl.sos.state.mo.us/00/soslibra/slref/ mostdoc /history/governor/govbio18-txt%09%09%2B> Accessed 17 Sept. 1999.

15 Bartels, Carolyn M. The Battle of Pilot Knob 1864. n.p., 1995. page 23.

16 Suderow, Bryce A. Thunder In Arcadia Valley: Price's Defeat, September 27, 1864. Cape Girardeau, MO: The Center for Regional History and Cultural Heritage, 1986. page 77.

17 Ibid, 141.

Comment: Suderow and most reports claim only 50 African-American defenders at the fort. An extensive review of the Cyrus Peterson papers in the possession of the Missouri Historical Society by the author has confirmed 66 African-American names and 95 white civilian volunteers. The author's work is in the possession of Fort Davidson State Historic Site, Pilot Knob, MO.

18 Ibid, 100.

19 "Latest From Pilot Knob: Authentic Details, Heroism of General Ewing." Daily Missouri Democrat [Saint Louis] 3 Oct. 1864: 1

20 Peterson, Cyrus A. & Joseph Mill Hanson. "General Thomas Ewing's Great Military Feat Fifty Years Ago." Thomas Ewing Collection. Ohio Historical Society Item PA Box 41-9, circa 1914. page 12.

21 J. Thompson, 292

2   Suderow, 138-140.

23 Peterson & Hanson, General 13.

24 Latest, DMD 3 Oct. 1864, 1

25 Suderow, 123.

26 Ibid, 124.

27 Peterson, Cyrus A. & Joseph Mill Hanson. Pilot Knob: The Thermopylae of the West, New York, NY: Neale Publishing, 1914. page 224.

28 Ibid, 253.

29 Ibid, 253 .

30 Russell, Theodore Pease. A Connecticut Yankee in the Frontier Ozarks. Columbia, MO: University of Missouri Press, 1988. page 177.

31 OR 1-41/1: 450.

32 Castel, Albert. General Sterling Price And the Civil War in the West, page 218.

33 J. Thompson, 293.

34 Suderow, 133.

35 Ibid, 135.

36 J. Thompson, 294.

37 Peterson, Cyrus A. & Joseph Mill Hanson. Pilot Knob, page 212.

38 Suderow, 123.

39 Ibid, 141.

40 Peterson, Cyrus A. & Joseph Mill Hanson. Pilot Knob, page 175.

41 Suderow, 120.

42 "Serenade to General Ewing and His Companions." Daily Missouri Democrat [Saint Louis] 7 Oct. 1864: 1.

43 Monaghan, Jay. Civil War on the Western Border: 1854-1865. Lincoln, NE: First Bison Books, 1984. page 315.

44 Ron Smith Unpublished Research E-Mail to author 12 Mar 2001

[Story of Thomas Ewing III, 26 Feb 1896 found by Smith in the Thomas Ewing Collection, Library of Congress, box 214].

Comment: If you are browsing and see this, refer to chapter five and footnoted text marked 27 for part of the story.

CHAPTER VIII

FOR THE DEFENSE

The most important trial General Ewing took part in was his defense of Doctor Samuel Mudd and two other alleged Lincoln assassination conspirators. Lorie Ann Porter and others have suggested that after the trial, "much political tar remained" which ruined his career.[1] Defending Doctor Mudd, however, was not political suicide, but supporting a hated President could well have been. President Andrew Johnson had his enemies, but the Ewing family did not count in their number. Instead, General Ewing and his father helped the President on a regular basis. His defense of Mudd and Ewing's support of President Johnson, which was more damning to the General than the Mudd Trial prove Ewing would set aside business to once again defend the US constitution.

Following the Battle of Pilot Knob, General Ewing saw that the war was concluding and that he needed to salvage his business interests and political career. He traveled to Kansas in January 1865, while the state senate debated to elect a US Senator. Clearly, Lane perceived him as a threat because he snubbed him. Several state senators attempted to unite Lane's opposition behind Ewing and apparently even offered "lukewarm followers of Lane" one thousand dollars for their votes. Unfortunately for the General, on January 13, 1865, James Lane once again was elected Senator.[2] Therefore, Kansas held no immediate promise for the future civilian.

General Ewing then traveled to Washington, D.C., in February 1865, and sought a private meeting with President Lincoln. He wished to resign his commission. During the meeting, Lincoln asked that he stay on duty and offered him the permanent rank of major-general. Ewing declined, but Lincoln refused to accept that for an answer and placed his letter of resignation in a pigeon hole on his desk. It was found there after the assassination.[3]

The assassination traumatized the nation. Secretary of War Edwin Stanton and Radical Republicans saw treason and spies everywhere. The attack on Secretary of State William Seward confirmed this in their minds. As the investigation concluded, ten people stood alleged to have treasonously conspired to assassinate the President and other officials. One, John Wilkes Booth, lay dead. John Surratt fled to Canada. Eight citizens of the United States remained to be tried. General Thomas Ewing accepted the task of defending three of the alleged conspirators: Doctor Samuel Mudd, Samuel Arnold, and Edman Spangler (figures 13, 14, and 15 respectively). How did he become the lead attorney for their defense, did he defend them well, and did this cause him political harm?

A connection between the Ewing family (although not specifically with General Thomas Ewing) and the Mudd family through friends has been traced, and Ewing may have defended Mudd as a family favor. There was also a belief among certain officials that the assassination was a Catholic plot and that the Ewing family chose General Ewing to protect Mudd as a fellow church member.[4] General Ewing never explained his decision. While such reasons are possible, so, too, is the Ewing family belief in fair play, which Ohio Supreme Court Judge Charles Sherman (the General's father) said he learned at the knee of the Honorable Thomas Ewing.[5] Possibly the General saw it as an act of contrition after Order Number 11 or as a stand against Radical Reconstruction. The truth may never be known, but might be as simple as that he believed it his duty as an officer of the court and that Frances Mudd, wife of Samuel, entered his Washington office and asked his help, knowing him to be a good lawyer and a distinguished general.[6]

Figure 13. Doctor Samuel A. Mudd.
Source: Library of Congress.

Figure 14   Samuel Arnold.
Source: Library of Congress, Prints & Photographs Division.
Reproduction # 4A4020

Figure 15 (Bottom). Edman Spangler (in hand irons).
Source: Library of Congress, Prints & Photographs Division,
Reproduction # 4A40214.

One point is certain. Ewing was not chosen by his family to defend Mudd because a sacrificial lamb was needed in this politically embarrassing trial. That viewpoint would only develop among a few younger family members in later years, if they admitted the General's participation in the trial at all.[7] The Ewing family, especially the senior Thomas Ewing, would never allow any family member to suffer political suicide. Three events demonstrate that fact. When Sherman came under attack for his actions at Shiloh, the entire family began a campaign against his detractors.[8] When Secretary of War Stanton criticized Sherman's lenient peace terms, the Ewings again came to his defense.[9] During Andrew Johnson's administration, the old Senator talked his son out of taking two controversial cabinet posts and, instead, offered himself to the President. To attack a Ewing incurred the wrath of the entire clan. Besides, the General was not the only lawyer in the family. In 1865, the Honorable Thomas Ewing still practiced constitutional law and helped his son prepare the legal defense of these defendants.[10] If the family saw the trial as a potential problem, there is no doubt that Daniel Webster's old friend would have stepped into the judicial arena once more.

On May 9,1865, at 10:00 AM, the military tribunal commenced at the Old Penitentiary Building, located at the Washington Arsenal in Washington, D.C.[11] It was headed by Major-General David Hunter, a long time friend of President Lincoln. All of the defendants requested counsel and were allowed another day to secure one. The next day, the court read the charges and specifications against them.

> Charge.- For maliciously, unlawfully, and traitorously, and in aid of the the [sic] existing armed rebellion against the United States of America combining, confederating, and conspiring together - to kill and murder - Abraham Lincoln - President of the United States of America, and Commander-in-Chief of the Army and Navy thereof;

Andrew Johnson, now Vice-President of the United States aforesaid; William H. Seward, Secretary of State of the United States aforesaid; and Ulysses S. Grant, Lieutenant-General of the Army of the United States aforesaid...and in pursuance of and in prosecuting said malicious, unlawful, and traitorous conspiracy aforesaid, and in the aid of said rebellion...together with said John Wilkes Booth and John H. Surratt, maliciously, unlawfully, and traitorously murdering the said Abraham Lincoln...and maliciously, unlawfully, and traitorously assaulting, with intent to kill and murder, the said William H. Seward...and lying in wait with intent maliciously, unlawfully, and traitorously to kill and murder the said Andrew Johnson...and the said Ulysses S. Grant...[12]

Over the next two days, Doctor Mudd introduced General Ewing and Frederick Stone as his counsel. Samuel Arnold and Edman Spangler also chose the General to defend them. After the tribunal approved of counsel for the defendants, the defense immediately began when all of the accused challenged the jurisdiction of the commission. When that failed, they all asked for separate trials. Again, failure. They then pled "not guilty" to both the charge and specification. With the preliminaries over, the trial began in earnest.[13]

In the next month and a half, the government presented assorted evidence to support claims of a conspiracy and to link these eight people to terrorism. For example, the prosecution contended that they were involved in placing bombs under Libby prison, in buying infected clothing to introduce yellow fever to Baltimore, and in plotting to burn New York City.[14] After the more fanciful accusations had been uttered, the prosecution settled down to attempt to link the defendants to each other and to the conspiracy. The prosecution concluded on May 23, and the defense concluded on June 10. The next twenty days consisted of arguments and rebuttals.[15]

Ewing's clients varied in degrees of guilt. As to Mudd's guilt, Frederick Stone, his other attorney, made this statement after Mudd's death:

> The court very nearly hanged Dr. Mudd. His prevarications were painful. He had given his whole case away by not trusting even his counsel or neighbors or kinfolk. It was a terrible thing to extricate him from the toils he had woven about himself. He had denied knowing Booth when he knew him well...He had been even intimate with Booth.[16]

Arnold was proven to not be in Washington that fateful night and that most likely saved him from the gallows.[17] He also cooperated with the authorities by giving them a statement against the other conspirators.[18] Stagehand Spangler merely had conversed with a man (Booth) he admired for about a minute and a half and then held his horse briefly at the stage door before someone else could be found to hold it.[19] A connection outside of Ford's Theater between the two men could not be proven. So, the General's most difficult defense concerned the doctor, who had been in contact on several occasions with Booth, and who claimed that he did not recognize Booth when he showed up one night at his door because he wore a beard. Such a thin disguise for an accomplished actor! To be in theater, Booth would have learned hair coloring, make-up, and the use of false noses and false teeth, but Mudd's story is that Booth relied on a fake beard. How did the General keep this man from his appointment with the hangman?

General Thomas Ewing and Senator Reverdy Johnson (Mary Surratt's attorney) starred in the defense. The other attorneys could not match their forensic abilities, and since

Ewing's men all escaped the executioner, he indeed outshone the others. The former Kansas Supreme Court Judge constantly challenged the prosecution throughout the trial, despite being almost constantly overruled by commission. In brief, he simply did not give up on his defense.

He attacked repeatedly and at length that the charge and specifications were not a legitimate single charge. Conspiracy to kill the President and others, killing the President, attempting to kill William Seward, and lying in wait to kill Grant and Johnson, Ewing insisted, were four separate charges. He argued that the charges be split and that the tribunal advise the defendants if they were charged with one or all of the specifications. As part of this, Ewing also argued that the charge, as written, did not relate to any known law on the books and wanted to know where it could be found.[20] No law spoke of "traitorously murdering." The Hunter Commission could, and ultimately did, invent their own definition of what that term meant. In attempting to answer General Ewing's question, the Assistant Judge Advocate, John A. Bingham, stated: "One crime all round, with various parts performed."[21] Throughout the trial, the commission insisted that there was one charge and one specification, yet upon sentencing, they split it into various parts.

General Ewing challenged the jurisdiction of the tribunal. Impassioned by this violation of his client's Constitutional rights, he argued that the military did not have the legal authority to try the case as civil courts were still open. The reason the military was hearing the case at all was due to an Attorney General's opinion given to the President that the military had authority in the case since Washington was under martial law.[22] Had he not given that opinion, President Andrew Johnson most likely would not have established the commission. Ewing argued that martial law did not exist as the war was over, thus negating the commission's jurisdiction. Ewing condemned the court, stating: "You are no court under the Constitution."[23]

If any argument could backfire in this trial, Ewing's challenge of martial law could have done so because of his imposition of Order Number 11. The commission was not inclined to hear the defense side of any issue. The trial was a political show, and the defense was there serving as a façade of fairness; otherwise, more of Ewing's objections would have been sustained. Still, if there was one way to attack the integrity of the commission, it was in Ewing presenting this argument. Yet, such was his rage over this attack on the Constitution, that he could do no less. To this day, his attack forms the basis of the Mudd family appeals of Doctor Mudd's conviction. Candida Ewing-Steel, Doctor Mudd's current lawyer and great-great-granddaughter of General Ewing, commented: "Without this argument, we probably could not be proceeding now."[24]

Doctor Mudd had been the most difficult to defend as he had met with Booth several times and conspired to kidnap the President and his cabinet. Fortunately for the Doctor, General Ewing successfully proved several witnesses to have defective memory at best or at worst to have made perjurious statements. In particular, two witnesses, William A. Evans and Louis J. Weichmann, gave incorrect statements. Evans, who by his own words was "on the verge of insanity," invented several key points concerning the Doctor being at Mary Surratt's house and his initial meeting with the doctor in 1850.[25] Likewise, Mudd benefited from a befuddled Weichmann. Weichmann, accompanied by John Surratt, met Mudd and Booth walking together on the street. The four retired to Booth's room at the National Hotel for cigars and drinks. Weichmann then reported that Booth and Mudd had several private conversations together at that time. He reported this occurred about January 15, 1865.[26] Luck protected the doctor again. The meeting had occurred on December 23, 1864. General Ewing knew that and used it to his client's advantage by proving that Doctor Mudd never traveled to Washington between December 23, 1864, and March 23, 1865.[27] The one man who could link Mudd, Surratt, and Booth together and send the doctor to the gallows lacked the credibility necessary for even the extralegal commission to order an execution. On June 30, 1865, the tribunal sentenced Edman Spangler to six years

136

of hard labor, while Doctor Samuel Mudd and Samuel Arnold received life sentences.[28] Mudd escaped the noose by one vote. However, General Ewing did not stop defending his clients.

Immediately after the trial, prior to Mary Surratt's execution, General Ewing was once again in the lead for the defense. In Reverdy Johnson's absence, he prepared a writ of habeas corpus for her to be brought by two other attorneys before a circuit judge and then the President. The military tribunal had recommended the death sentence be commuted to life imprisonment for Mary Surratt, but President Andrew Johnson (figure 16) later insisted that he never saw the writ and that Judge Advocate General Holt withheld it from him.[29]

According to Ewing, Johnson did see the writ prepared by him. After reviewing the writ, the President suspended habeas corpus in her case and ordered the execution.[30]

The next year, the United States Supreme Court decided a similar case, Ex Parte Milligan. The Milligan decision held that if the civil courts were open in a territory of the United State not engaged in insurrection, then any citizen arrested in said territory must be tried before a civil court.[31] Exactly the argument General Ewing had pursued in this case! Had the Supreme Court had the chance to hear Mudd's defense, the ruling possibly would have favored the Doctor by holding that the case should have been tried in a local or federal court in Maryland, as he allegedly committed his offenses in Maryland.

The conspirators should have been charged simply with treason, which is against the Constitution, and tried in federal court in the District of Columbia or Maryland. Furthermore, a murder charge in Washington could have been filed. Since they conspired to commit treason by killing the President, the federal statute on felony murder (generally, that if one person commits murder during the commission of a felony all of the participants in that felony could be charged with murder) should have been filed against them. Why then resort to a preposterous charge in a tribunal with questionable jurisdiction?

Maryland and the District of Columbia were both below

the Mason-Dixon Line. They were slave territories which had not seceded from the Union. As such, each shared a disproportionate share of Southern sympathizers. In the postwar atmosphere, the possibility existed that jurors with Southern leanings would vote to acquit. Secretary of War Stanton and other Radical Republicans needed a conviction and that was not guaranteed in civil court. Historically, their fears proved correct. In 1867, John Surratt was brought back from Europe to stand trial. The jury failed to reach a unanimous decision.[32] While John Surratt walked freely from the courthouse, Doctor Mudd languished in a federal prison on Dry Tortugas, seventy-five miles west of Key West, Florida.

Ewing continued his activities in defense of his clients and worked on the issue at the presidential level. Reverdy Johnson was left with the task of seeking writs of habeas corpus in Florida.[33] On July 4, 1868, President Johnson granted amnesty to those who had fought in the rebellion. Mudd's lawyers immediately applied for another writ of habeas corpus, basing their argument on this presidential order. Judge Boynton refused to grant it, but did permit Mudd's lawyers to seek relief in the United States Supreme Court.[34] Although General Ewing received no credit for obtaining presidential pardons for Mudd, Arnold, and Spangler, his close ties to President Johnson must have played some part in the decision Johnson made on March 1, 1869. In the pardon, Johnson wrote that Doctor Mudd's implication in the assassination amounted to performing actions according to his physician's oath and being involved only after the fact.[35] Upon notification of the pardon, the Supreme Court dismissed the case. After serving almost five years, Doctor Mudd returned to Maryland.

General Ewing saw his duty as an officer of the court and carried it out to the best of his ability. Some suggest that certain members of the tribunal did not want to embarrass the General by imposing the death sentence on his clients and that is why Mudd escaped the hangman.[36] To reduce his efforts to favoritism belies the General's legal abilities. The thought that accepting this case ruined him politically fails to recognize the obvious. While it may have hindered the ambitions of a Republican, General Thomas Ewing had no intention of seeking the favors of the Radical Republicans who controlled Congress. He intended to thwart their efforts at Reconstruction of the South. After the death of Lincoln, his contempt for Radical Reconstruction led him to the Democratic Party.

The years 1864 to 1869 were a watershed period in the life of General Thomas Ewing. He had been victorious in battle and had become a renowned general. His defense of Mudd put his name in almost every newspaper in the land for weeks at a time. Instead of returning to Kansas, he started a new law practice in Washington. Some of his dealings in Kansas finally began to pay off, little by little. The entire family had made friends with the new President, Andrew Johnson. Most importantly, he worked in earnest for Democratic Party causes. Ewing looked upon the Democrats as the party closest to his principles. It was a first step towards election to the Senate. Thomas Ewing, Jr., was on the verge of success.

To accomplish his goal, General Ewing began modeling himself into a candidate. He had many of the requirements already. Still, one detraction was his Roman Catholic faith. Non-Catholics would still express concern some ninety-five years later about Papal interference in politics when John F. Kennedy ran for President. If Ewing had not begun slipping away from the faith before this period, a few events would have accelerated it during this time. His mother died early in 1864 and, most likely, with that the last vestige of practicing the Catholic faith died also. His wife, Ellen, converted to Catholicism when marrying Tom with no intention of practicing it. When she joined him in Leavenworth, this daughter of a Protestant minister became a member of the First Presbyterian Church.[37]

The General apparently decided, as his biography suggested, either that God was not the property of any one religion or that overtly practicing Roman Catholicism while attempting to become a United States Senator would hinder his career (his father only converted to the faith on his death bed, although he attended Catholic services regularly).[38]

Figure 16. Seventeenth US President, Andrew Johnson. Source: Photograph No. NWDNS-111-B-4138; (Mathew Brady Studio); "Hon. Andrew Johnson, Tenn., President, U.S.;" Office of the Chief Signal Officer; National Archives at College Park, College Park, MD.

Being Roman Catholic was political suicide and both men knew it. Instead of practicing Catholicism, he attended Presbyterian services with his wife.[39] With the religion issue behind him, he was ready to join the fight against Radical Reconstruction by running for office. Unfortunately for the General, the President needed his services, which meant that his goal would have to wait.

General Ewing immediately established a law practice with his father when he arrived in Washington in February, 1865. At different times, Senator Orville Browning and General Charles Ewing partnered with him in his practice.[40] While the General began to build his business, he also immersed himself in backroom politics. For example, he became a member of the Congressional Democratic Executive Committee although he was not a member of Congress.[41] In 1866, General Ewing and his father busied themselves with insuring that Hugh Ewing received Senate confirmation of his post as Minister to the Hague. As early as the fall of 1866, the two Thomas Ewing's dedicated paragraphs in many letters to Minister Ewing that they anticipated impeachment of the President. That, however, occurred late in February, 1868.

The well-known story is simple, but the connection to the General or his father has been often overlooked. Congress, led by the Radical Republicans, passed the Tenure of Office Act, which generally said that the Senate must approve the removal of government officials from office once they have been confirmed into that position. President Johnson wanted to remove Secretary of War Stanton and fired him. Stanton responded by refusing to leave office. Congress reacted swiftly. After months in which the President and Congress stayed at loggerheads over several issues dealing with Reconstruction, on February 25, the House of Representatives notified the Senate that they had voted impeachment for the President violating the act.

The day prior, President Johnson tried to submit the name of the Honorable Thomas Ewing to the Senate as the Secretary of

War. General Ewing had been the President's choice, but the senior Ewing considered the post so controversial at that point that it could ruin his son's career. He talked Thomas, Jr., out of the position.[42] Unfortunately, the President failed to present this appointment to the Senate in a timely manner. Had he announced his nominee's name immediately following his declaration to remove Stanton, a wisely chosen nominee would have dulled the blow to the Radicals. Instead, the President acted as "Sir Forcible Feeble," in General Ewing's words.[43]

When the impeachment trial began, the General worked behind the scenes once again by giving the President advice on several counts. Determined as always to maintain the proper legal procedures, the General encouraged President Johnson to comply with a clause in the Tenure of Office Act, which required he notify Congress within twenty days of a removal. Attorney General Henry Stanbery wrote the letter, which, for a short time, turned public favor to the President.[44] After Stanton countered the letter and public opinion wavered, the President needed a defense team and, for that purpose, conferred with his cabinet, as well as such people as Reverdy Johnson and General Ewing. He then chose a defense team comprised of both Democrats and Republicans, led by Stanbery.[45] Stanbery had to resign as Attorney General and again the President turned to the General as a possible candidate to replace him in the cabinet, except that the nomination never materialized.[46]

As the impeachment continued, General Ewing struck out on the campaign trail, not for himself, but for Democrats generally, and, more specifically, to beat the drum for the President. On March 8, 1868, he wrote to his brother, Hugh, from Bradford, New Hampshire, as he stumped for the Democratic candidate for Governor: "...I must own that more than half my time is taken up with the affairs of the nation and of friends, thus reducing very greatly my efficiency at money making."[47] At a public debate in Washington's Judicial Square, Benjamin F. Simpson, who declared that General Ewing was no friend of his, gave this account of a Ewing torchlight speech:

[H]is face and frame showed that he was
swayed by the most intense excitement.
The torches had burned low, and their
dying and spasmodic flare threw a weird
light over the scene. Ewing seemed to
have expanded into colossal proportions,
and with a face darkened by passion, and
a voice that could be distinctly heard
above all the noise and din of the crowd,
was denouncing the leaders of
impeachment, their plot to destroy the
Government, their allies and abettors,
the public sentiment that demanded the
removal of Johnson, and predicting all
kinds of disasters should the President
be impeached...It has been a marvel to
me ever since that he did not so inflame
the Southern adherents of Johnson that
night as to cause bloodshed.[48]

General James Blunt, who also disliked Ewing, was
with Simpson and considered the speech the most passionate
he had ever heard.[49]

General Ewing did not cling to Johnson solely in the
hopes of rewards. When he spoke of the Constitution, he
spoke with a passion. When he spoke of a citizen's rights, he
spoke as he believed and, as the Mudd case proved, would
challenge those who would violate those rights at every turn.
Ewing firmly believed Radical Reconstruction was against the
Constitution, and he had decided to do whatever he could to
prevent or limit inflicting this upon the South. The General
believed:

[Reconstruction] would proscribe the
whites of the South and make the negroes
the rulers; that their government would
have to be propped by bayonets and must

fall when the support was withdrawn; that it would prove a vast burden on the North and destructive to the South, and as wholly unconstitutional.[50]

Not only did Reconstruction disenfranchise those men who fought for the Confederacy, it forced other sweeping changes on the Southern populace at the point of a bayonet. First, the Southern states were divided into five military districts. Second, military courts could try citizens for crimes, although Federal civil courts were open. Third, the military served as an occupying army by maintaining order and enforcing federal laws. Fourth, the act required each Southern state to enact a new state constitution, which would allow black suffrage. Finally, the act required the state to approve of the fourteenth amendment to the US Constitution before the state was readmitted to the Union.[51]

Shortly after the impeachment trial, at the 1868 Democratic Convention, Ewing was met with loud applause when he gave voice to the disenfranchised South:

We earnestly wish to accomplish the purposes of the war as we understand them...the truly cordial, unconditional restoration of this Union...We have no sympathy for those purposes that have been falsely and dishonestly substituted by the Republican Party for the avowed .objective of the war...We care not for their dogma of negro suffrage; we abhor their measures of white disenfranchisement We look upon them as enemies of the Republic...[who] undermine and overthrow the settled foundations of our Government.[52]

General Ewing saw that once the South had been rehabilitated and military occupation withdrawn, the plight of the black populace would worsen. History has validated that fact. After all, he wanted freed slaves to have all the rights and liberties guaranteed others by the Constitution. He further believed that the disenfranchisement of white Southerners was not constitutional. Moreover, Ewing realized that Reconstruction was designed to keep one party in power, since, as long as Southern whites could not vote and Southern blacks could, the new Southern voters would continue to elect those (i.e., Republicans) who kept them in power.

To the ire of the Radical Republicans, the President had been successful in blocking some of their bills which penalized the Southern States. The Supreme Court also handed down some decisions against their agenda. Ex Parte Milligan, which held that citizens could not be tried by military courts when civil courts were functioning, had been recently decided.[53] Ex Parte Garland and Cummings v. Missouri were decided the month before impeachment began and both held that disenfranchisement by using test loyalty oaths was unconstitutional. Additionally, Reconstruction "by-passed the Constitution" by such means as requiring states to approve the Fourteenth Amendment and by denying the state the choice to decline it until it had been enacted by a two-thirds majority of states.[54] Not only was the Radical power base eroding away through Presidential vetoes and from Supreme Court rulings, recent elections were also bringing Democrats back to power in many states.

To counter these trends, a small group led by Senate President pro tem Benjamin F. Wade, House majority leader Thaddeus Stevens, and Congressman Ben Butler saw impeachment as a means to seize and keep power for the Republicans. The President had given them an excuse by removing Stanton. If the President could be convicted, Wade was next in line to be President (since Johnson had no Vice-President, this would have been possible under the

Constitution). Wade wanted to be President and saw this as a way to "achieve what he had little chance of gaining at the Republican National Convention in 1868."[55] Keeping his brother, Minister to the Hague Hugh Ewing informed of the political high jinks, the General wrote:

> ...I think if Wade gets in [the Presidency], the jig is up with the Democracy and conservatives for some years. The Rads will never let themselves get elected out of power after they get all the power in their hands.[56]

Wade's chances seemed strong, as conviction appeared certain. All the votes were counted beforehand, except one.

The vote on impeachment occurred on May 16, 1868, and the vote seemingly turned upon a single man, Senator Edmund G. Ross of Kansas. Ross was a Radical Republican newspaper publisher and former Captain in Ewing's regiment. He had denounced Senator James H. Lane for being too soft on the President.[57] Other Kansans voiced similar concerns. Ross was a Radical's radical

Many Kansans were decidedly Radical Republicans and strongly favored impeaching the President. On the other hand, Lane always supported him and his Reconstruction policies. As his feelings became known, Lane's most ardent supporters turned against him and old friends failed to call on him. Returning to Leavenworth in failing health, Lane believed his end neared. On July 1, 1866, the ill Senator, "(o)verworked, mentally deranged, [and] depressed by his cold reception in Kansas," placed a revolver in his mouth and pulled the trigger. The bullet traveled through his brain, yet he clung to life for ten more days."[58]

With the death of the flamboyant Senator, his Senate seat became vacant. Needing someone to complete the remainder of Lane's term, Governor Samuel J. Crawford turned to Edmund G. Ross because he was an educated activist. The former 11th Kansas major sided with Radicals on all occasions. He even voted to condemn the President for violating the Tenure of Office Act. That vote preceded the impeachment proceedings. However, as each Senator announced his decision before the impeachment trial began, only one remained silent. The new Senator believed the case must be proven for his vote. For the castigations Ross received after the vote, it would be inappropriate to fail to credit Ross for his decision. It was a brave stand. However, someone probably helped influence him.

Ross stated unequivocally that Republican Ben Butler tried to buy his vote.[59] Others tried to see that he would not be in town so that the President would lose by a fraction of a vote. Others wined and dined him. General Ewing, as a longtime friend, certainly made at least one attempt to convince the Senator of the Constitutional reasons for voting in favor of the President. No record exists of that meeting, except possibly in the long lost notes kept by the people the Radicals assigned to follow the undeclared Senator.

Regrettably, no smoking gun, no letter from Ewing to Ross, has ever been found arguing the President's case. However, two letters and a telegram exist from which such a connection may be inferred. In 1894, former Senator Ross wrote the General asking his assistance in obtaining a New York publisher for a book on the impeachment. Ewing's reply was favorable.[60] Besides asking for his help in editing the work, Ross wrote: "But your habitually candid, conservative judgment [sic] and strong common sense, upon which I have so many times implicitly relied in the past, peculiarly fits you to advise me, & I shall rely very much upon what you may suggest..."[61]

The strongest accusation that Thomas Ewing influenced his former military subordinate came from a man who would gladly be considered the enemy of either man, Dan R. Anthony. The Leavenworth mayor telegraphed Ross when the vote became known: "Your vote is dictated by Tom Ewing, not by your oath. Your motives are Indian contracts and greenbacks. Kansas repudiates you as she does all perjurers and skunks."[62] Still, these documents contain no absolute proof that Ewing convinced Ross to vote in favor of the President.

Given the friendship forged in the crucible of war between Ewing and Ross and the fact that Ewing supported the President and, like all other vote counters, knew that Ross had not declared his vote, a strong probability exists that Ewing tried at least once to sway the Senator's vote. Both men acted out of duty and Ross's act was described as "the most heroic act in American history."[63] If one believes General Ewing's eloquent Constitutional arguments swayed the Senator, that belief by no means minimizes the fact that, on one fateful day, Edmund G. Ross stood alone.

Defending the President cost Ewing, some personal funds. By supporting the President, Ewing "made a large sacrifice...enough certainly to free his actions from the slightest suspicion of any other motive than conviction of duty."[64] Even in the eyes of Radical Republicans such as Simpson and Blunt, he gained in stature. Although the payments trickled into his coffers, Ewing made money defending Doctor Mudd.[65] Throughout his life, he believed that the trial helped his reputation.[66] His support of Mudd might have been questionable to some Radicals, but easily forgivable. However, they could never forgive his support of President Johnson. His support of the President hurt any chances he may have had at the 1868 Democratic Convention because the desire for another Johnson term was very low. Likewise, it prevented him from receiving a nomination to a federal post in either party's next administration. Nevertheless, he had begun positioning himself for the time when his party would obtain power and become a voice for Democratic Party principles.

Chapter VIII Endnotes

1 Porter, Lorie Ann. "Not So Strange Bedfellows: Thomas Ewing II and the Defense of Samuel Mudd." Lincoln Herald (1988): 91-101. page 98; Lackey, Mike. "The Ewings of Ohio." Lima News 1996. Internet Edition.

2 Stephenson, Wendell Holmes. The Political Career of General James H. Lane. Topeka, KS: Kansas State Historical Society, 1930. page 148.

3 Hannahs, Harrison. "General Thomas Ewing, Jr." Collections of the Kansas State Historical Society 1911-1912, Vol XII (1912): Topeka, KS: State Printing Office. page 280.

4 Porter, 95.

5 Lackey.

6 Porter, 100.

7 Porter, 98.

8 Fellman, Michael. Citizen Sherman: A Life of William Tecumseh Sherman. Lawrence, KS: University Press of Kansas, 1995. page 104.

9 Thomas, Benjamin P. and Harold M. Hyman. Stanton: The Life and Times of Lincoln's Secretary of War. New York, NY: Alfred A. Knopf, 1962. page 415.

10 Steel, Candida Ewing. "Re: Boynton Decision." E-mail & Attachment of Ewing's letter to his father dated 7 July 1865 to Walter E. Busch, 26 Oct. 1999 10:16 AM.; Library of Congress. General Thomas Ewing, Jr., Papers. TEJ to TE 7 July 1865.

11 Jones, John Paul, ed. Dr. Mudd and the Lincoln Assassination: The Case Reopened. Conshohocken, PA: Combined Books, 1995. page 264.

12 Pitman, Benn. The Assassination of President Lincoln and the Trial of the Conspirators. New York, NY: Funk & Wagnalls, 1954. page 18.

13 Ibid, 22.

14 Ibid, 62, 53-55.

15 Ibid, xxi.

16 Higdon, Hal. The Union vs. Dr. Mudd. Chicago, IL: Follett Publishing Co, 1964. page 208.

17 Pitman, xxi.

18 Ibid, 234.

19 Ibid, 105.

20 Ibid, 245.

21 Ibid, 247.

22 J. Jones, 263.

23 Pitman, 354.

24 Steel, Candida Ewing. "Mark-Up Notes to For The Defense." E-Mail with Attachment to Walter E. Busch, 28 Oct. 1999, 1011 hours.

25 Pitman, 323.

26 Ibid, 324.

27 J. Jones, 240.

28 Pitman, 248.

29 Castel, Albert. The Presidency of Andrew Johnson. Lawrence, Kansas: University Press of Kansas, 1979. page 34.

30 Library of Congress. [LOC] General Thomas Ewing, Jr., Papers. TEJ to TE 7 July 1865; Steel Re: Boynton.

31 J. Jones, 266.

32 Ibid, 265.

33 Ibid, 149.

34 Ibid, 149-151.

35 Ibid, 265.

36 LaForte, Robert S. Thomas Ewing, Jr. Unpublished Notations, circa 1990. page 4.

37 Spencer, Joab. "The Methodist Episcopal Church, South, In Kansas--1854 To 1906." Collections of the Kansas State Historical Society. 1911-1912, Vol XII. Topeka, KS: State Printing Office, 1912. page 151.

38 Clark, S. J. Record of Fairfield County: A Biographical Record of Fairfield County, Ohio. New York, NY: S.J. Clark Publishing, 1902. page 477.

39. "Gen. Ewing's Religion." Lancaster Gazette 19 June 1879.page 2.

40. Clark, 479.

41 LOC, TEJ to H. Ewing 4 May 1868.

42 Libert, Don. "High Crimes and Misdemeanors." Fairfield Heritage Quarterly, Vol. 13 No.   4 (Fall 1991). Lancaster, OH: Fairfield Heritage Assoc. page 5.

43 LOC, TEJ to H. Ewing 8 Mar. 1868.

44 Trefousse, Hans L. Andrew Johnson: A Biography New York, NY: W.W. Norton & Co., 1991. page 306.

45 Ibid, 317.

46 Warner, Ezra J. Generals In Blue: Lives of the Union Commanders. Baton Rouge, LA: Louisiana State University Press, 1964. page 147.

47 LOC, TEJ to H. Ewing 8 Mar. 1868.

48 Simpson, Benjamin F. "The Wyandotte Constitution."

Kansas Historical Collections 2 (1875-1880): 236-247. Topeka, KS: KSHS. page 244.

49 Simpson, 244.

50 Clark, 479.

51 Castel, Presidency 107.

52 "The Democratic Convention." New York Times 7 July 1868. page 1.

53 Castel, Presidency 100.

54 Ibid, 108.

55 Bonadio, Felice. North of Reconstruction: Ohio Politics, 1865-1870. New York, NY: New York University Press, 1970. page 154.

56 LOC, TEJ to H. Ewing, 8 Mar. 1868.

57 Kennedy, John F. Profiles in Courage (Memorial Edition). New York, NY: Harper Perennial, 1964. page 135.

58 Stephenson, 159.

59 LOC, Ross to TEJ 18 Aug. 1894.

60 Kansas State Historical Society. "The Thomas Ewing, Jr., Papers" (microfilm edition), manuscript division, Kansas State Historical Society, Topeka., TEJ to Ross 26 July 1894.

61 LOC, Ross to TEJ 10 July 1894.

62 Harrington, Arthur Elliot. Edmund G. Ross: A Man of Courage. Franklin, TN: Providence House Publishers, 1997. page 76.

63 J. F. Kennedy, 132.

64 Clark, 479.

65 LOC, TEJ to TE 7 July 1865.

66 LaForte, 4.

CHAPTER IX

THE GENERAL'S LAST BATTLE

Tell me, Ewinged winds that on the platform roar,
Do ye not know some spot where cheek will win no
more?
Some rare and pleasant dell, some valley in the West,
Where flat money falls and Tom will get a rest?
The soft wind dwindled to a whisper low
And sighed to answer, "Yes- O--hi--o!

Unknown, Geneva Times, 12 June 1879

After discussing the artwork, "Order No. 11," Lew
Larkin and other art historians concluded that it was such a
strong propaganda painting that its use by General Ewing's
political foes ultimately destroyed his public career.
Concerning the 1879 Ohio governor's race, Larkin specifically
concluded: "Through his pen and brush, Bingham had stopped
Ewing's promising political career."[1] Albert Castel stated: "In
1879 he waged an unsuccessful campaign in which Bingham's
painting, 'Order No. 11,' was used against him."[2] Likewise,
Goodrich asserted: "More copies of 'Order No. 11' were
circulated...when the crucial votes for governor were counted
Thomas Ewing had fallen by a 3 percent margin."[3] It seems
most historians recording the General's political demise have
relied on the same sources Larkin used and reflections
recorded by Curtis Rollins, the son of Bingham's closest friend.
In doing so, they have relied on the easy explanation.

Further research has been suggested, yet not detailed. David March commented: "(T)here is no evidence to support the well-known story that the artist's pen and brush defeated Ewing for governor of Ohio in the 1870's."[4] A reference in <u>Missouri Sketch Book</u> reported that John McDermott conducted an extensive study of the legend, but found no basis in fact.[5] Yet, a review of McDermott's work provided few revelations regarding his research (which he limited to the 1875 and 1877 campaigns) and little more than a conclusion that: "We are forced to accept the will for the deed."[6] The propaganda hindered General Ewing in only one way, which had no bearing on any election campaign he fought. By identifying alternate and better sources, the truth that Order Number 11 was anathema to Ohio Republicans, because it was seen as being inflicted on Democrats in the name of a Republican government, and that the Ohio Democratic party loss in 1879 was due to other reasons will be revealed.

The controversy begins with the 1868 Democratic Convention which was held several months prior to Bingham completing his art piece. Allegedly, the climax of :

> ...[the Order No. 11 painting controversy] was reached in the Democratic national convention, which began its session in Tammany Hall on July 4, 1868...At the convention Thomas Ewing, who had become a Democrat, and whose residence was Ohio, was slated for nomination for Vice President, and had secured enough delegates to command the nomination ...the convention adjourned...In that interim Montgomery Blair, who wanted the nomination for his brother, Frank P. Blair, Jr.,...got a job printer in Ann Street to strike off a large number of copies of "Order No. 11," signed "Thomas Ewing,"...The result was the immediate

destruction of Ewing's chances for the
second place...[7]

Such a political embarrassment would have certainly
commanded the attention of the <u>New York Times</u>, but the
paper was silent on such an act. Thus, it must not have
occurred. A review of the events proves the fallacy of that
story.

Two days after delivering a very successful
Independence Day speech to a national convention of Union
soldiers and sailors at Cooper Institute in New York, Ewing
was called unexpectedly to the platform before the Democratic
Convention at Tammany Hall.[8] He stressed the necessity of
union between Northern and Southern Democrats against
"those who are plotting to overthrow the Union of the States
and our constitutional form of government..."[9] At no time did
he mention anything about being a candidate for either the
office of President or Vice-President.

As the convention proceeded with business and the
roll-call votes for President were tallied, on the third and fourth
ballots, the Georgia caucus declared one of its votes for
Thomas Ewing, Jr. He had received a half vote on the second
ballot also, but he really was not a threat to the main
nominees.[10] In the end, the nod went to Horatio Seymour, who
did not have a war record and that would be a problem when
facing General Grant.

Next, the nominations for Vice-President began. In
due turn, the Kansas delegation, represented by Charles Blair,
entered into nomination "a man who is celebrated as a judicial
officer and distinguished as a statesman, and whose military
career was the very impersonation of chivalric and knightly
honor...the name of Gen. Thomas Ewing, Jr., of Kansas." A
letter was then read from the Soldiers' and Sailors' Convention
recommending General Ewing as Vice-President, if a
candidate from the East was nominated for the Presidency.[11]
The caucus from Maine seconded Ewing's nomination. As the

154

nominations drew to their conclusion it was obvious that Frank P. Blair had considerable support. The Kansan, Charles Blair, then stood up and asked for Ewing's name to be withdrawn from consideration "at his instance." [12]

As there were no breaks between the nominations and this withdrawal of Ewing's name, the account in the Joseph Mudd book is obviously inaccurate. The General's ego would have allowed him to accept the nomination for President, as he believed only a Democrat with a war record could stem the Grant steamroller, but had no intention of placing his name behind Seymour's.[13] Ewing withdrew for two reasons. Most importantly, Blair had stronger support. Second, Ewing considered the Seymour ticket a losing one against General Grant. He did not want his first post-war venture into public office defeated. Editorializing upon the convention's choice, the New York Times opined:

> The nomination of Blair was the final Democratic catastrophe. The Soldiers' and Sailors' Convention had urged the name of Gen. Thomas Ewing, Jr., of Kansas, for the Vice-Presidency. The Convention ignored this expressed preference, and chose to insure defeat by saddling their ticket with the Blairs. At least so said street gossip... [14]

"Order No. 11" had been conceived by Bingham as early as 1865, but he did not complete it until November 1868.[15] The convention took place four months earlier. While it may have been partially finished, the Blairs would have had to have a photograph taken of the unfinished work in Kansas City, had it developed, then sent it on an express train to New York, if they became aware of a Ewing threat a few days before the convention started. The story clearly stated the Blairs used the painting and not the text of the Order.[16] They could have had the Order's text printed, but surely the New

<u>York Times'</u> gavel to gavel account would have reported such an overt attempt to influence the nomination. Therefore, "Order No. 11" must not have been a factor.

In 1870, the General closed his law offices in Washington and moved back to Lancaster, Ohio. His original plans were to move to either Kansas or Ohio, but his father's ill health and his father's gift of the Ewing family home weighed heavily in his decision. Ewing took the small fortune of about two hundred thousand dollars he earned as a lawyer and lobbyist with him.[17] He immediately began to immerse himself into Democratic politics. In 1871, some politicos considered him a threat as a possible candidate for Governor. George Caleb Bingham related that Ohio congressmen wrote him asking for copies of the picture, "plainly stating they wanted to use them against Ewing." The engraver, working on a plate from which copies could be made, had yet to complete his work, but Bingham would not give up on this opportunity to harass the General. Instead, he made a small photograph of the picture and sent it to the congressmen for their use.[18] Given the photographic capacities of cameras, film, and reproduction technology in the nineteenth century, it is doubtful that a photograph without the glass negative would have been a sufficient propaganda tool.

If the painting and its associated propaganda could have hurt the General, it occurred in this attempt. However, Ewing was defeated without the aid of "Order No. 11."[19] Two years later, the <u>Toledo Commercial</u> newspaper's obituary of the Honorable Thomas Ewing briefly mentioned the accomplishments of his family. With regards to the General, the paper reported: "(H)is name has recently been before the people of this State as the choice of the Democracy for Governor, though he was defrauded of the nomination by the friends of Mr. [George W.] McCook."[20] In a speech given a little more than a month after the 1871 Ohio Democratic State Convention, General Ewing explained:

But, recently, a prominent Democrat of

Lancaster has seen fit to revive the assertion in a modified form [that I am the nominee of the party and not McCook], in a letter attacking the nominee and the platform. That gentleman is so connected with me by ties of friendship and family that I feel it is proper for me, not only to disavow all knowledge of that letter before its publication, but to say that I regard its statements...as an unkindness and an injustice to me.[21]

From the above two statements, the politicking to be the gubernatorial nominee was obviously intense, and McCook seemingly deprived Ewing of a nomination. Therefore, the painting's harmful use was distinctly possible, since the political jousting occurred within the Democratic Party. Still, other reasons should be considered.

If the propaganda associated with the painting ever affected Ewing, it would have been in the backroom politics that occurred when Democrats met to nominate a new candidate. General Ewing was a Republican in the war and imposed Order Number 11 on Southerners, i.e. Democrats. As represented by his Democratic enemies, Ewing was a man who turned his back on the Democrats to support Republican politics during the war and, in doing so, committed atrocities against fellow Democrats in the name of the people of Kansas. However, the alternate argument considered the fact that Missourians were slavers standing against the Union and committing atrocities against blacks and fellow Northerners. Since Missouri politics was not of great concern in Ohio, it could have affected his nomination but probably did not. A more plausible reason may have been Ewing's support for soft money. Another equally logical reason was that he had returned to Ohio only one short year before the convention and had yet to develop wide-ranging support within the party. A myriad of Ohio issues could have swayed delegates more easily than the display of a fictionalized painting of Ewing on horseback overlooking criminal acts committed by the Red Legs he despised.

Hoping to profit from his artistic commentary on Red Leg atrocities, Bingham borrowed money to purchase the engraver's prints of "Order No. 11." The prints were ready in 1872, but the economy dipped into a depression by 1873. Bingham's dreams of a tidy profit at the General's expense were crushed.[22] General Ewing was not cooperating, either. Since he lost the nomination in 1871, he did not run for any office. Instead, he busied himself by assisting in a new draft of the Ohio Constitution (the 1873 draft was never ratified). This work kept the General in the political arena but well in the background. Thus, Bingham never fully recovered his money from this ill-timed business venture.

General Ewing worked hard in 1875 for the Democratic party, the Democratic gubernatorial nominee, and Greenback ideals. He ardently opposed the 1875 Congressional act that called for the resumption of specie payments (paying gold or silver money in exchange for the paper money issued during the war), and spoke for the Ohio Democratic Party throughout the state in a series of debates with Governor Stewart Woodford of New York. Ewing believed that paper money was every bit as good as gold and that the government should distribute more of it as the country's economy expanded. In a debate at Tiffin, Ohio, General Ewing quipped on the absurdity of the resumption act:

> The gentleman, in reply, burst out...that that sweaty old coin could be put through the fire and would come out bright and pure; whereas the sweaty greenback might be put in the fire and would be entirely consumed. True--but if the sweaty greenback were put into the fire

158

and consumed, you could get another from the treasury in its place. Besides, what under heavens should the people want to put their money in the fire for?[23]

By 1877, Ewing again decided to try for a political office. Being elected to the House of Representatives seemed to hold good opportunities. Therefore, he prepared for the task. If "Order No. 11" had even been a small issue in the 1871 Democratic nominations, Ewing wanted to overcome that issue once and for all. The "Order No. 11" conflict reflected the ongoing friction between the so-called Charcoals (wartime radical members of the Democratic party) and Claybanks (the moderates and conservatives). The moderates and conservatives did not appreciate the need for total or hard war, and Bingham's letters to newspapers in the 1870s continued to stir up those old feelings.[24] General Ewing attempted to sidestep this argument in the upcoming caucus by obtaining the support of his former superior, General Schofield. Schofield, who was then serving as the superintendent of West Point, responded to Ewing's request on January 25, 1877.

The newspapers published Schofield's letter on February 21. Ewing's former superior summarized the situation on the border as one that either required more soldiers to police the area or the removal of the guerrilla supply source (i.e., rural population). Schofield reported that since he was ordered to send as many troops as possible to support General Grant at Vicksburg, the second solution seemed the only plausible one. He also reported that although General Ewing had issued the Order, it had his and President Lincoln's support.[25]

The artist swiftly responded with a letter denouncing the attempts to clear Ewing of any wrongdoing. Bingham admitted that both sides had committed atrocities, but blamed Red Legs and Union soldiers for the bulk of them. In the letter, he also commented that he was in Kansas City at that time, hoping to have the order rescinded.[26] However, as a private letter clearly stated, he was there only to press his claims for his house.[27]

Unfortunately for the General, his efforts to justify his war actions began at a time when Bingham was attempting to press war claims for the damage to the Thomas residence and he willingly vented his anger to the press.[28] The claim that the General had to change his ambitions from that of being Governor to being a congressman from his home district is not supported by the evidence.[29] McDermott researched the 1875 and 1877 Ohio Democratic Conventions and concluded that the controversy had no effect on the General's ambitions to be Governor, as he had not been a candidate for the office.[30] Furthermore, a conclusion can be reached that the propaganda had little effect on Ewing's immediate ambitions, as he was elected to Congress in November 1877.

Bingham followed Ewing to Congress as bad luck. The artist presented his claims for war damages to his house to Congress in March 1878. With Bingham's help, the Washington Sentinel published a "series of lengthy, weekly, front-page articles [against the] new leader of the Democracy."[31] During this period in Bingham's life, his son, Rollins Bingham, rebelled against his father. Bingham's personal letters to his friend, James S. Rollins concerning this episode in his life "are obsessive, repeating information, ruminating... Paralyzed into inaction in the face of his son's rebellion, he could take action only against Ewing."[32]

Ewing ignored Bingham's attacks and busied himself in the country's affairs. He successfully led the fight to amend the species resumption by reissuing greenbacks as people turned them in for hard money. Later, Secretary of the Treasury John Sherman admitted that it would have failed without such an amendment. Congressman Ewing also believed in silver coinage and offered several bills on that subject. He may have even been responsible for authoring a bill which later became the Bland-Allison Act of 1878. This law directed the government to buy $2 to $4 million dollars of domestic silver

160

monthly to produce coinage. This act was, therefore, responsible for the government minting what are now called "Morgan" silver dollars.[33] The General further "proposed to retire the national bank currency and fix by constitutional amendment the volume of the greenback currency and its enlargement in proportion to the annual percentage of increase in the population." While failing that, he successfully established legislation prohibiting the use of federal supervision at state elections.[34]

Throughout his pursuit of political offices and his later career in Congress, General Ewing continued his efforts in either land or railroad speculation. Most of his concerns dealt with coal land in the Ohio counties of Perry and Athens and the Atlantic & Lake Erie Railroad (A&LE). On paper, the A&LE had a debt of about $3 million in 1873. At that time, Thomas Ewing and his future political rival, Charles Foster (figure 17), joined its board of directors. The following year, Foster and Ewing were two parts of a triumvirate responsible for all of the railroad's major decisions. In April, Ewing went on hiatus from his A&LE duties to serve for a year in the Ohio Constitutional Convention.[35]

The 1873 Constitutional Convention caused him to neglect some duties with the railroad and, surprisingly he also introduced a proposition contrary to the business needs of all railroads. He presented an amendment to article 15 of the proposed constitution, which read that: "No person, while elected to, or holding office...shall accept any gratuitous or commuted service from any railroad company."[36] Considering that the use of gratuities in Kansas by the LP&W was known to him and that he, personally, had to buy Lane's support, Ewing's amendment certainly is a change.

While the convention considered the important issues of state, the nation suffered considerably from a depression. Although hard times meant tight money, the owners of the coal companies led by Ewing decided to attempt completing the railway. With that group's backing, on March 18, 1875, Ewing

161

was unanimously elected the A&LE president. He changed the name to Ohio Central Railroad (OC) and issued approximately $7 million more bonds. Ewing strove to build the OC on massive credit, similar to the way in which other railroads were constructed at the time. He sought out the money of European investors, as well as farmers and townspeople along the route. Unfortunately the depression continued and the line stayed in the red. By July, 1877, the OC was in receivership.[37] Seven thousand stockholders along the road had to pay more money to satisfy the debts of the company under Ohio law. According to a <u>Cincinnati Daily Enquirer</u> report, Foster, while serving on the board, allegedly received over $6 million in bearer bonds (which entitled the holder to money even if the railroad failed). The article continued that Foster "has lately come into possession of the road at one- twentieth its original costs..." Furthermore, Foster never accounted for those bonds, but the paper continued that the stockholders then had to pay him more money.[38] Ewing's management of the OC would become an issue in the 1879 election, and, to a lesser degree, Foster's role was also analyzed.

Ewing's ambitious plans for the A&LE failed for several reasons. First of all, the directors were inexperienced in railroad building, which cost time and money due to bad business decisions. For example, rather than concentrating on building the railroad in sections, many sections were abandoned in various stages of construction. Second, Ewing pushed his ideas on the board in attempts to salvage his land holdings. These decisions were not always the best ones for the railroad. Despite that fact, "It is far from certain that different management or different policies would have led to success..." Third, the ongoing depression kept the OC from attracting financiers. However, in some respects, the A&LE board was visionary. More specifically, "Ewing's integrated approach toward industrial development served as a model for a syndicate..." In 1879, the Thomas Syndicate acquired the remains of the OC. The railroad quickly turned a profit of

$126,399.08 in 1881 and, by 1883, the enterprise's coal holdings in the Hocking Valley were valued at over $4 million.[39] The collapse of the OC hurt Ewing sufficiently, so that it would take him years to fully recover.[40]

After his resignation from the bankrupted railroad, the time had arrived for the General to push towards his life's goal. Rutherford B. Hayes had become President after serving as Governor of Ohio, and the political gossip hinted that Thomas Ewing could be the next Democratic candidate for President, if he first became Governor. The Democrats had two leading candidates, but there were two other names in consideration. Governor Richard M. Bishop and General Rice were the main two candidates, while Senator Allen G. Thurman and Ewing received mention as dark horses. The St. Louis Daily Globe-Democrat reported that by June 3, neither candidate had a majority and that Ewing, who also offered the hope that Greenbackers would support his nomination, had support in both camps.[41] Bishop's supporters abandoned him first, and, on June 4, General Ewing, absent in Washington, received the Democratic nomination as Governor, and General Americus V. Rice became the candidate for Lieutenant Governor.

The hope that General Ewing would also be endorsed as the candidate of the Greenbackers was short-lived. The same day, A. Saunders Piatt received the National Greenback Labor party nomination, but General Sherwood and some others "bolted the action of this Convention and issued a call for another one to meet in Toledo on the 26th inst., presumably in the interest of the Ewing-Rice Democratic ticket."[42] Nothing resulted from Sherwood's act, and the campaign became a four party race (which also included a small Prohibitionist contingent). In that race, Ewing's strongest opponent was Charles Foster, the Republican candidate.

Figure 17. The Honorable Charles Foster. Ewing's rival in the 1879 Ohio Governor's Race. The National Archives lists the date on this photo between 1860 and 1865, but Foster was not a Congressman until the 1870s, so the date estimated appears to be in error. Source: Photograph No. NWDNS-111-B-1927(Mathew Brady Studio); "Hon. Charles Foster, Ohio;" Office of the Chief Signal Officer; National Archives at College Park, College Park, MD.

General Ewing's campaign troubles started before he received the nomination. Instead of representing himself at the convention and swaying the crowd, and possibly some Greenbackers as well, he relied on others to handle the affair. Next, he suggested removing the head of the party's executive committee, John Thompson, and replacing him with Colonel Len Harris. Ewing received a telegram from the convention asking whether "a row" was desirable at that time. Ewing replied that he desired party harmony, but stood by Harris.[43]

In the meantime, the sick and aging Bingham continued to spew his hatred. On June 6, the <u>Kansas City Mail</u> announced: "Order No. 11 is beginning to boom in Republican organs and in Democratic papers of the [Samuel J.] Tilden persuasion."[44] For every Bingham attack, General Ewing received support from other politicians in Missouri. Former Missouri Governor B. Gratz Brown questioned Bingham's motives in a June 17 open letter. Bingham prepared a response, but on July 6, was stricken with cholera and the aged artist-statesman died the following day.[45] His vengeance, however, rose from the grave for one more attack on the General.

Bingham's son, who was now reconciled with his father, found the artist's response and allowed it to be published. In his letter, Bingham stated Generals Richard C. Vaughn, Odon Guitar, and Frank Blair (Blair had helped obtain President Lincoln's approval of the order) as indicating the Order was a horrid mistake.[46] The open letter that covered five-sixths of page five allegedly resulted in a controversy, which Ewing supporters had to justify and Foster constituents publicly referenced.[47] While this may have occurred in Missouri, the story was different in Ohio from Larkin's history.

The controversy obviously had some press. In researching this debate, Larkin and other historians exclusively cite Kansas City, Saint Louis, and Washington papers. Only McDermott bothered to research the Ohio papers, but limited his research to the years 1875 and 1877. The Ohio papers largely ignored

165

this Missouri issue. It had always been an issue in Democratic circles while considering the General for nomination. After Ewing received his party's nod, no Democrat cared to speak publicly about the controversy. On the other hand, the Republican newspapers could not use it. The newspapers with Republican leanings felt that General Ewing's conciliatory efforts to heal the rift between North and South deserved to be labeled as "Confederate." They could not on one hand say that he sympathized with rebels and then on the other condemn him for committing the allegedly most harsh act of the war against Southerners. One other source indicated that the unpleasantness General Ewing experienced concerning the Order involved only Democratic politics. Thomas Ewing commented in an 1890 reception in Kansas City: "I have been pelted by the Democratic party on this account; and the charge that I was cruel to my fellow beings while in a position to command is galling."[48]

Several Ohio papers, including one written in German, were reviewed in preparation for this analysis. To say that the newspapers never referenced the Order would not be true. Bingham's hate crusade simply was no longer a story to Ohioans. Not one of the letters being discussed in Missouri was published in the papers reviewed. Additionally, the articles reviewed from the time of Ewing's nomination through the election displayed a virtual lack of interest in "Order No. 11."

Immediately after his nomination, the Cincinnati Weekly Gazette recorded the story of the Washington, D.C., serenade to the General upon his receiving the news. Senator George G. Vest of Missouri, who served the affected border yet also supported Ewing, declined to speak on behalf of the General, as he felt it would alienate his supporters. The report continued: "The order is one which the Republicans have always stoutly defended, but which Missouri Democrats and Democrats in other portions of the South, have always bitterly attacked."[49] Next, the Lancaster Gazette, an anti-Ewing newspaper, said this of the controversy:

> Most of our readers have doubtless heard a great deal about a certain Order No. 11, issued by Gen. Thomas Ewing...Few of them, however, have an adequate idea of the character of the order...It was a measure which at the time of its issue was generally approved by Union men, but which the rebels and copperheads of that day characterized as the act of a monster in human form, and which to this day in all the region affected by it calls down upon the head of Gen. Ewing their fiercest execrations and denunciations.[50]

On the same page, the Gazette recorded a news brief from Cincinnati. That brief, in its entirety, stated that: "Ewing claims that Order No. 11 ought to be barred off because he is not running for Governor of Missouri."[51]

The Sandusky Weekly Register published one article about how the General conducted the war in Pettis County. The article concerned events not associated with the depopulation, but identified Ewing as the author of the "famous" (not infamous) Order Number 11. An unidentified reporter for the Sedalia Eagle interviewed T. J. Johnson of Sedalia, who was "well acquainted with Gen. Ewing." Johnson asserted that he had a confrontation with some of the General's soldiers. Reportedly, the soldiers stole from the home of a Major Gentry, a "true Union man." In conclusion, Johnson alleged that Ewing was "the meanest kind of thief."[52] A check of Civil War records found that a Major William Gentry served as the commanding Union officer of the Fifth Provisional Regiment Enrolled Missouri Militia stationed at Sedalia.[53] General Ewing and his troops were also near Sedalia chasing Colonel Shelby during 1863, but the article did not specify any date. Normally, he would not have been in the Sedalia area, since the town was outside his area of command. A search of the State Historical Society of Missouri did not find a copy of the <u>Sedalia Eagle</u> to compare the story. Therefore, Mr. Johnson's story was possible. However, the story reads as gossip, folklore, or contrivance.

Ten Ohio papers were reviewed for any evidence of Order Number 11, and the four instances cited above were the only ones found published from June to November 1879. While other papers may well have published criticism of Order Number 11 and perhaps even Bingham's letters, the main papers appear to have been largely silent. The politicians in Ohio knew it to be a Democratic issue to be used against Ewing before any nomination. In the 1879 gubernatorial race, Republicans wanted to prove Ewing's "Confederate" tendencies, not his oppression of Confederates. If "Order No. 11" was not a main issue, what other ones factored into his defeat?

While the two candidates refrained, as gentlemen, from abusive attacks upon the other, the Ohio newspapers relished in name calling. Generals Ewing and Rice, despite their war records, were labeled "Confederates," while Charles Foster had the nickname of "Citizen Foster," due to his lack of military record, and "Calico Charlie," as he sold fabrics during the war. Another sobriquet Ewing received was "Tissue Thomas," for his ability to bring monetary woes to the public.[54] Some mud slinging of note included: Ewing's voting record in Congress; Ewing's land deals; an alleged secret deal between Tilden and Ewing, and the General's religion.

One of the first attacks against the "Confederate" Democrats involved the dismissal of a federal employee. Captain S. S. Blackford had been a disabled Union soldier who served as Captain of Capitol Police until he was fired. In his place, General Ewing recommended former Confederate General Allaback, who received the appointment.[55] The Republican newspapers sought to sway Union soldiers away from the General with this attack. Another accusation made was that Ewing had recently visited "a Shylock or two" in New York and had been ordered to stop his Greenback rhetoric if he wanted their money.[56] Supposedly, another Ewing failing was in his support of the Wood Tariff, which the Republican papers contended would have paralyzed industry.[57] The Lancaster Gazette also claimed Ewing reneged on a promise of a government appointment to a "prominent Democratic organizer." Instead, the Gazette continued that he only obtained two appointments, and one of those went to his nephew, Tom Ewing.[58]

Besides Ewing's Ohio railroad deals, any land deals with which he had been involved became fertile ground for criticism. Other Ewing business concerns involved the Ohio Great Vein, Dover, Sunday Creek Valley, Carbon Hill, and Brier Ridge mining companies, as well as the Athens Coal and Coke Company. The Gazette mentioned that several people, including farmer-investors, made money, at least on paper, in these ventures.[59] Another article related that Ewing ran up the debt of the OC while he was the president and received payment for his services while people like Charles Foster lost money.[60] The account certainly differed from the Democratic version which claimed that Foster held millions in bearer bonds.[61] With so many people in his home district reportedly losing money in alleged land schemes, how could these citizens elect him to Congress twice within the previous three years?

Supposedly, another damning allegation was that the General had ties to the last Democratic candidate for President, Samuel J. Tilden. Ewing had not initially backed Tilden in his presidential ambitions during the 1876 Democratic Convention, but after Tilden became the nominee, Ewing endorsed him. The Republican press spoke of a Tilden-Ewing alliance in the 1879 general elections. When he won the election, Ewing supposedly was to hand Tilden the votes of the Ohio caucus and, in turn, become the Vice- Presidential candidate. Moreover, the General's campaign efforts in Ohio were to receive contributions from the Tilden machine.[62] Ewing admitted meeting Tilden in New York, but insisted that they did not discuss contributions or the next presidential campaign.[63] Besides, if the General won the election, the Presidency itself would be within reach. That was his desire.

One final issue may have hindered Ewing in his gubernatorial endeavors. Ewing never left the Roman Catholic Church. When his father died in 1873, his faith must have been in question by family members. Ellen Sherman, during her preparation of The Memorial of Thomas Ewing, had numerous family members and friends submit letters attesting to the Senator's good works and death bed conversion to the faith. Absent from all these testimonials is a single letter from the General or his wife. Thomas Ewing, Jr., supplied a few letters written to him expressing sympathy, but no letters from him appeared in his sister's book. Even references to him are limited. One possible conclusion from this would be that his pious sister truly believed he had strayed from the path.

Amazingly, for a time when many viewed Catholicism as another worldwide conspiracy, few articles concerned his faith. Equally surprising is that the Lancaster Gazette came to the General's defense, but with a twist. The Gazette joined The Ohio State Journal in contending that the Democratic papers were raising the question of religion, but the Republican papers were not. Together they accused the Zanesville Signal of trying to blame the Republicans. The article observed that Republicans had placed Generals Sherman and Sheridan, both Catholics, at the head of their armies. The Journal's article concluded: "If you want to find a bigot, you must go in search of a Democrat." To this, the Gazette added that the General was not a member of any church, but "the family's usual place of worship here is the Presbyterian church."[64] This may have affected some votes, but other factors added to the Democratic collapse.

General Ewing was outspoken in his views while his

opponent was apparently less inclined to speak on national issues. When slavery had been an issue, Ewing and his father were willing to compromise. On his own without the cooling waters of wisdom from his father, the political firebrand would not yield on his issues. He had even spoken out against his party on occasion. This opened him up to rebuke. His appointments on various boards of directors were public ones mainly due to the fact that he represented the business to the community while others, like Charles Foster, stayed in the background. As such, disgruntled stockholders could accuse him of fraud. His positions, while seen as welcoming Greenbackers back to the party, alienated other party members.[65] Ewing's Greenback message depended on hard times, but the specie resumption (with Ewing's amendments) was successful and that allayed the discontent of many who may have supported him. The Ohio Democrats hoped for the Ewing-Rice ticket to provide a cohesive bond to the party; however, some fractionalization occurred because the General wanted to run the campaign his way. Elder Ohio politicians saw him as an upstart. His message of elections free of military presence had more ears open to it in the South than in Ohio. Another criticism he leveled for the national press was President Hayes's frequent use of the veto.[66] Instead of concentrating on Ohio issues, he acted as if preparing for a run on the national ticket. With so many other issues, "Order No. 11" never amounted to a problem in Ohio.

Several papers predicted Republican wins as early as the day after the Democratic convention. On June 12, Ewing's home town newspaper commented: "(W)e shall be disappointed if it [the Foster ticket] does not sweep the State by a majority of 25,000 in October."[67] By October, a newspaper supportive of Ewing wrote of his "gallant canvass of Ohio," as if searching for some enthusiastic phrasing.[68]

On June 18, the New York Tribune described how the Republicans could win in Ohio. The article stated that Ohio had 660,000 voters, with the Republicans having a slight edge.

If the people became apathetic, the Democrats would win. Yet, the author predicted this would be a lively campaign. In 1878, the Republicans won by a plurality of only 3,150 votes. Democrats hoped that Ewing would add the 38,000 votes the Greenbackers received in that election to their column and give the party victory. However, the article suggested that 70,000 people failed to vote in the 1878 election and most of them were Republicans, so 38,000 votes could still be a losing number. The article then showed that the Republican vote in October 1876 was over 317,000. By November, they commanded 331,000 plus votes. Come the October 1878 election, they received slightly more than 274,000 votes. On the other hand, the Democrats received over 314,000 votes in October 1876; climbed to more than 323,000 in November; and declined to almost 271,000 votes in October 1878 (all losing numbers). The Prohibition vote fell between 1,500 and 2,000 votes in the 1876 elections, but had grown to 5,600 votes in 1878. The Greenback party had not even been a factor in the October 1876 election, but received over 3,000 votes that November. In October 1878, they received over 38,000 votes. Greenback candidates generally received their support from people who would otherwise ally themselves with the Democrats. The Republicans could beat Ewing, if they mobilized their entire vote. Thus:

> Gen. Ewing will be fortunate if he succeeds in getting as many as 5,000 votes from men who have been Republicans on account of their Greenback proclivities. But he will be a thousand times more fortunate if he does not lose twice as many votes of Democrats who detest his heresies and dread the destructive Communistic spirit to which the party appeals in his nomination.[69]

The Republicans had won every major election since 1876, except the 1877 race for Governor. During that dull election (if the <u>Tribune's</u> analysis was accurate), the Republicans lost anywhere from 67,000 to 80,000 votes due to a lack of interest. Therefore, Ohio voted Republican more often than not.[70]

It was to be a good year for the Republicans and a bad one not only for Ewing, but for Democrats in many states. Ohio's citizens went to the polls on October 14, and, the next day, the <u>Cincinnati Weekly Gazette</u> estimated Republican gains of 7,500 votes and a win by 20,000 votes.[71] However, the full story unfolded as the election results from Ohio and other states were finalized. The Democracy received a pounding everywhere. In New York, Massachusetts, Pennsylvania, Illinois (including the city elections in Chicago), Minnesota, Connecticut, Nebraska, New Jersey, Kansas, Michigan, and Wisconsin, the Republican juggernaut rolled to victory. Only in the Southern states did the Democrats win. The Ohio gubernatorial race produced the following results: for Foster, 336,261 votes; for Ewing, 319,132 votes; for Gideon Stewart (Prohibition Party), 4,145 votes; for Piatt, 9,072 votes; and for John Hood, 547 votes. There were also 13 votes for various other people. The General lost by 17,129 votes.[72]

"Thus, a switch of about 1 1/2 percent of the votes would have elected Ewing" is an accurate remark.[73] However, it does not consider the Greenback vote, which most conceded would have voted for Ewing had the party not nominated Piatt. That would have reduced Foster's lead to 8,057 votes. That comment also fails to account for the fact that Ewing received the second highest number of Democratic votes for the leading state office on the ticket since 1876. Likewise, it does not account for the high Republican turnout. Had Ewing tried harder to unite Democrats, appease the old guard, and stress state issues, he might have won, but it was all an up hill battle.

Finally every Bingham-Ewing researcher, heretofore, has failed to recognize the strength of the Republican victories throughout the Northeast and Upper Midwest, which surely affected the Ohio campaign. "Republican Victories Everywhere...[and] Scarcely a grease spot left of Democracy" are two ways the Lancaster Gazette described the Republican regional landslide.[74] President Rutherford B. Hayes thought the election soundly defeated "two great issues--inflation and states' rights...[and] interpreted it also as Ohio's stamp of approval on his administration."[75] With the strength of the Republican victory across the nation, the General's loss by only three percent of the vote showed proof of his vigorous campaigning efforts.

The "Order No. 11" art controversy started when George Caleb Bingham first publicly displayed his work. On more than one occasion, Bingham had to defend his portraiture of Union soldiers as being brutal.[76] Prior to finishing his art work, Bingham did not attack Ewing. When Ewing became a potential candidate in 1868 for the second highest office in the land, Bingham stayed silent. In 1871, Bingham sent one photograph to some Ohio Congressmen. It may have factored into the nomination, but probably did not since there was only one photo and the engraver's copy was not ready. By 1876, Ewing prepared to run for a Congressional seat and had General Schofield prepare a letter defending the order. Bingham responded in the Missouri papers. Since the General was elected to Congress, it obviously did not affect that campaign either. In 1878, Bingham struck out against Ewing, but only because the artist was seeking war damage reparations. "Order No. 11" also did not affect Ewing's campaign during the Ohio 1879 Governor's race, although Bingham once again raised the issue. It seems that the only times the controversy arose was when Bingham wanted to stir up the old hatreds, defend his art work when critics attacked it, receive money or when Ewing asked Schofield for support . The shine on the Missouri artist's political armor is dulled, although his artwork will shine forever. In the end, General Ewing lost not as a result of a propaganda campaign on the

Missouri issue of "Order No. 11," but because the people of Ohio preferred the Republican stand on state and national issues.

Chapter IX Endnotes

1 Larkin, Lew. Bingham: Fighting Artist. Point Lookout, MO: School of the Ozarks Press, 1971. page 323.

2 Castel, Albert. Civil War Kansas: Reaping the Whirlwind. Lawrence, KS:University Press of Kansas, 1997. page 228.

3 Goodrich, Thomas.Bloody Dawn: The Story of the Lawrence Massacre. Kent, OH: Kent State University Press, 1991. page 178.

4 March, David D. The History of Missouri, Volume II. New York, NY: Lewis Historical Publishing, 1967. page 943.

5 Edom, Clifton C. Missouri Sketch Book: A Collection of Words and Pictures of the Civil War. Columbia, MO: Kelly Press, 1963. page 121.

6 McDermott, John Francis. George Caleb Bingham: River Portraitist. Norman, OK: University of Oklahoma Press, 1959. page 148.

7 Mudd, Joseph A. With Porter, In Northern Missouri. Iowa City, IA: Camp Pope Bookshop, 1992. page 444.

8 "The Soldiers' and Sailors' Convention: The Convention Listens to A Speech." New York Times, 5 July 1868. page 1.

9 "The Democratic Convention." New York Times 7 July 1868. page 1.

10 "The Democratic Convention." New York Times. 8 July 1868. page 8.

11 "The Democratic Convention." New York Times. 10 July 1868. page 1.

12 "The Democratic Convention." New York Times. 10 July 1868. page 8.

13 Bonadio, Felice. North of Reconstruction: Ohio Politics, 1865-1870. New York, NY: New York University Press, 1970. page 163.

14 Democratic, NYT 10 July 1868, 8.

15 McDermott, 140.

16 Mudd, 443-444.

17 Taylor, David G. "Hocking Valley Railroad Promotion in the 1870's: The Atlantic and Lake Erie Railway." Ohio History Vol. 81 No. 4 (Autumn 192): 263-278. Columbus, OH: Ohio Historical Society. page 265.

18 Rollins, C. B., ed. "Letters of George Caleb Bingham to James S. Rollins, Part V." Missouri Historical Review Vol. 33 No. 1 (1938): 45-78. Columbia, MO: State Historical Society of Missouri. page 70.

19 McDermott, 145.

20 Sherman, Ellen Ewing. Memorial of Thomas Ewing of Ohio. New York, NY: Catholic Publication Society, 1873. page 127.

21 Speech of Gen. Thomas Ewing, Jr., at Capitol Square, Columbus, Ohio, August 11, 1871, np., nd. page 1.

22 Larkin, 272, 276.

23 Lee, J. V., ed. Joint Discussions between Gen. Thomas Ewing, of Ohio, and Gov. Stewart L. Woodford, of New York on the Finance Question. Columbus, OH: np, 1876. page 100.

24 Simonds, May. "Missouri History As Illustrated By George C. Bingham," Missouri Historical Review Vol. 1, No. 1 (1906-1907): 181-190. Columbia, MO: The State Historical Society of Missouri. page 182.

25 Schofield, John M. "Gen. Ewing's Missouri Order." Missouri Republican [Saint Louis] 21 Feb. 1877: page 5, col. 4. ; Neely, Mark E. Jr. ""Unbeknownst" to Lincoln: A Note on Radical Pacification in Missouri during the Civil War." Civil War History: A Journal of the Middle Period Vol. XLIV No. 3, Kent, OH: Kent State University Press, 1998, pages 212-216.

26 Bingham, George Caleb. " Scorcher, Gen. Bingham on Order No. 11." Daily Missouri Republican [Saint Louis] 26 Feb.1877: page 5, col. 3 & 4.

27 Rollins, 62.

28 Rash, Nancy. The Paintings & Politics of George Caleb Bingham, New Haven, CT: Yale University Press, 1991. page 212.

29 Larkin, 300.

30 McDermott, 148.

31 Ibid, 149.

32 Rash, 214.

33 LaForte, Robert S. Thomas Ewing, Jr. Unpublished Notations, circa 1990. page 5.

34 Clark, S. J. Record of Fairfield County: A Biographical Record of Fairfield County, Ohio. New York, NY: S.J. Clark Publishing, 1902. page 481.

35 D. Taylor, Hocking 269.

36 Ohio, State of. The Official Report of the Proceedings and Debates of the Third Constitutional Convention of Ohio. 1873-1874. Cleveland, OH: W. S. Robinson And Co., 1873. page 68.

37 "Ewing's Wildcat Road." Cincinnati Weekly Gazette. 27 Aug. 1879. page 1; D. Taylor, Hocking 276.

38 Untitled. Cincinnati Daily Enquirer 6 Oct. 1879: Page 4 Col. 1. page 4.

39 D. Taylor, Hocking 278.

40 Clark, 480.

41 "The Outlook In Ohio. "St. Louis Daily Globe-Democrat 4

June 1879. page 1.

42 Untitled. Lancaster Gazette 12 June 1879: Page 2 Col. 2.

43 "Ewing, Thompson and the Central Committee Chairmanship." Columbus Daily Democrat, 9 June 1879. page 1.

44 Untitled. The Daily Mail [Kansas City, MO] 6 June 1879: Page 2 Col. 1.

45 Larkin, 311.

46 Bingham, George Caleb. "Bingham-Brown." Kansas City Daily Journal. 25 July 1879: 3.

47 Larkin, 322.

48 Clark, 479.

49 "The Campaign: How Gen. Ewing's Nomination is Received." Cincinnati Weekly Gazette. 11 June 1879. page 1.

50 "Order No. 11." Lancaster Gazette 3 July 1879. page 2.

51 "Political Notes and News." Lancaster Gazette 3 July 1879: Page 2 Col. 4.

52 "Gen. Tom Ewing: How He Ran the War in Pettis County." Sandusky Weekly Register 16 July 1879. page 5.

53 OR 1-22/1, 636.

54 "Reemelin's Ranting.," Lancaster Gazette 18 Sept. 1879: Page 3, Col. 2.

55 "Fine Business for a 'Union' General." Lancaster Gazette. 26 June 1879. page 2.

56 Untitled. Lancaster Gazette 3 July 1879: Page 2 Col 2.

57 "Political Notes and News." Lancaster Gazette 14 Aug. 1879: Page1 Col. 4.

58 "General, Read This!" Lancaster Gazette 21 Aug. 1879. page 3.

59 "Col. Mulberry Ewing." Lancaster Gazette. 31 July 1879, Sup. 4.

60 "Ewing and the Ohio-Central Railway." Lancaster Gazette. 11 Sept. 1879, 1.

61 "Ewing's Wildcat Road." Cincinnati Weekly Gazette. 27 Aug. 1879, page 3.

62 "The Alleged Ewing-Tilden Combination." Cincinnati Weekly Gazette. 9 July 1879, page 2.

63 "Ewing Speaks." Kansas City Daily Times. 7 Aug. 1879. page 2.

64 "Gen. Ewing's Religion." Lancaster Gazette 19 June 1879. page 2.

65 Jordan, Philip D. History of the State of Ohio Vol. 5: Ohio Comes of Age 1873-1900. Columbus, OH: Ohio State Archaeological and Historical Society, 1943. page 166-167.

66 Ibid, 166.

67 "The Ticket That Will Win." Lancaster Gazette 12 June 1879: Page 1.

68 Untitled. Cincinnati Daily Enquirer 6 Oct. 1879: Page 4 Col. 1.

69 "How The Figures Look In Ohio: The Republicans Can Win in a Fair and Square Fight." Cincinnati Weekly Gazette 18 June 1879. page 2.

70 "Review of the Ohio Election - And Estimates of The Results: Ohio Redeemed: False Financiers, and Democratic Misrule in the State." Cincinnati Weekly Gazette 15 Oct. 1879. page 1.

71 Ibid, 1.

72 Taylor, William A. with Aubrey C. Taylor. Ohio Statesmen and Annals of Progress from the Year 1788 to the Year 1900, Vol. I. Columbus, Ohio: Press of the Westbote Co., 1899. page 86-87.

73 Larkin, 323.

74 "Tuesday's Elections: Republican Victories Everywhere." Lancaster Gazette 6 Nov. 1879: Page 2 Col. 2.

75 Jordan, 168.

76 Larkin, 249-250.

CHAPTER X

AT THE SEAT OF CAPITALISM

Congressman Ewing was in his fifties and still capable of mounting another campaign, but he did not. When the General lost the gubernatorial election, he returned to Congress to complete the remainder of his term. After that, the Congressman retired from politics. In 1881, Ewing moved to New York City with his wife and family (figure 18) and established a law practice.

He never explained why he retired from politics. His loss hurt, but most likely he could have been reelected time and again to Congress. The party offered and he declined a chance at a third term. Philanthropic work now kept the General busy. He served as a trustee of a soldiers' and sailors' orphans' home from 1874 to 1878. From 1878 to 1883, he served as a trustee of Ohio University and, in 1881, acted as vice-president of the Cincinnati Law School.[1] Ohio was his home, and he easily could have busied himself with a legal practice, business venture, or any other projects. Probably the most logical conjecture for his leaving Ohio is that he desired to pay off some of the debts he incurred and what better place to do that than in New York City, the front offices of American capitalism. Therefore, the General and his family moved to Yonkers, where, with the Honorable Milton I. Southard, he established the partnership of Ewing and Southard located at 155 and 157 Broadway, New York.[2]

180

Figure 18. The General Thomas Ewing, Jr. Family. Left to right:
Thomas Ewing III (b.21 May 1862),
   Maria Ewing (b. 20 Nov. 1858),
   Ellen Cox Ewing (1833-1919),
   General Thomas Ewing (1829-1896),
   Hampton Denman Ewing (b. 18 June 1866),
   Mary Beall Ewing (b. 28 Sept. 1864),
   William Cox Ewing (b. 8 Oct. 1856).

   The web site with this photograph incorrectly records Ellen Cox Ewing's year of death as 1879. She died in 1919. Photo: Copyright 8 1998 Marilyn Price-Mitchell. Used with Permission.

Ewing had already been associated with many great men in nineteenth century America and, in 1883, a famous inventor briefly entered his life. Alexander Graham Bell had invented the telephone and received patent number 174,465 on March 7, 1876, for his efforts. The patent created a monopoly for the American Bell Telephone Company, which threatened telegraph companies' profits and prohibited them from creating like devices to transmit voice for the duration of its life. The patent became the most litigated one in history, with over 600 lawsuits attempting to void it. A company hired the General to find a loophole in the patent. While Ewing tried to prove that Bell had accomplished nothing unique or new, and that Bell's process "is false in theory and obsolete in practice; and all that is new in the device is utterly worthless."[3] Bell's patent survived his attack. Eventually, the patent withstood all six hundred lawsuits.

The next legal concern in the General's life involved his Kansas railroad dealings. The US Pacific Railway Commission began investigations in 1887 concerning corruption, missing funds, and unpaid debts of various railroads. The commission permitted Ewing to give a written statement and answer only a few basic questions in which he denied giving bribes during the passage of the Campbell Railroad Bill (while Ewing was the attorney for the LP&W). Evidence exists of some payments to politicians for their support of the LP&W's efforts, and those facts implicate the General in some of these payments.[4] Still, the General survived the testimony relatively unharmed. Due to findings of this and other similar commissions, Congress created the Interstate Commerce Commission, which was established the following year.

Early in 1891, the family in New York City gathered for a death watch. The family always came together in times of crisis, only this time the tragedy affected the nation. General William T. Sherman had contracted a cold and died on

February 14, as General Ewing and other family members surrounded his bed. They stayed in the bedroom for a short time and said a prayer for the departed. Then, General Ewing descended the stairs to announce to waiting reporters that Sherman's eternal march had begun.[5]

The General continued in his law practice with Southard until 1893, when he established the law firm of Ewing, Whitman, & Ewing, located at 41 Wall Street. Joining him in practice were his two sons, Thomas and Hampton.[6] The firm concentrated on business and patent law and the General's son, Thomas, later became a respected patent lawyer.[7] That same year, the elder Ewing held a seat on the Yonkers' Board of Trade (which later merged with the New York Stock Exchange). From March 1895 to July 1896, he also served as counsel to the New York City Building Department.[8] Old age was not slowing him down.

The General continued his social life by establishing the Ohio Society of New York in 1886. He then served as its president for three years.[9] He also continued public speaking, but turned his attention more to the history of the great struggle for freedom in the United States. Some of his speeches included addresses before the Sons of the American Revolution, a convention of soldiers at Marietta, Ohio, and at the unveiling of the Samuel S. Cox monument (Democratic US Representative from Zanesville, OH, who died in 1889). In 1890, the General delivered an address before the Kansas state bar association during which he commented about being harangued by Democrats for Order Number 11.[10] He finally had begun reflecting on his career with that speech. His next public reflection became an article in Cosmopolitan magazine regarding his organization of the Bolters. However, before the General could write a full account of his life, he suffered and unfortunate mishap. Around 10:30 A.M. on January 20, 1896, the Honorable Thomas H. Ewing, Jr., left his home at the Saint George Apartments, 223 East Seventh Street, to go to his law offices. He was enroute to an elevated rail station and stopped at the corner of Third and Eighteenth Streets as a northbound cable car passed. He then stepped onto Third and into the path of a southbound cable car. The General was thrown several feet and landed "heavily on his head." The police apparently thought the accident also involved criminality on the part of the cable car gripman John Kelly, as he was arrested.[11]

The head injury involved a subdural hematoma. During the night, the two attending doctors bore into his skull using a trephine and removed clotted blood from beneath the fracture. The article reads much like the accounts of Abraham Lincoln's death struggle, when doctors probed his wound with their fingers, which helped stimulate the breathing of the fallen President. Likewise, the General "rallied...but, despite the surgeons' efforts he gradually sank, until death came" on Tuesday, January 21, 1896.[12] New York City Hall flags were lowered to half staff. His funeral service was held at Yonkers First Presbyterian Church and serves as final evidence that he had left the Roman Catholic faith.[13] The former state Supreme Court Judge, Brigadier-General, Congressman, and businessman was laid to rest at Oakland Cemetery in Yonkers, New York.[14]

Chapter X Endnotes

1 Price-Mitchell, Marilyn. General Thomas Ewing. 1998.<http://www.sandcastles.net/thomas1.htm.> 1998. Accessed Aug. 1999.

2 "Death of Gen. Thomas Ewing." New York Times 22 Jan. 1896. 8; Ewing, Thomas, Jr. Opinion of Thomas Ewing on the Validity of the Claims of the American Bell Telephone Co., Under the Patent to A. G. Bell, of March 7, 1876.New York, NY: Francis & Loutrel, Stationers and Printers, 1883. page 1.

3. Ewing, Opinion 26.

4 "Thomas Ewing, Jr., and the Origins of the Kansas Pacific Railway Company."The Kansas Historical Quarterly, Vol. 42 No. 2 (Summer 1976): 155-179.Topeka, KS: Kansas State Historical Society. page 171.

5 Ewing, Joseph H. Sherman at War. Dayton, OH: Morningside House, 1992. page 172.

6 "Gen. Thomas Ewing Injured." New York Times. 21 Jan. 1896. page 1.

7 Steel, Candida Ewing. "Re: General Tom Ewing." E-mail to Walter E. Busch, 28 Sep. 1999.

8 Death of Gen. Thomas Ewing, 1.

9 Miller, Charles C. History of Fairfield County Ohio and Representative Citizens. Chicago, IL: Richmond-Arnold Publishing Co., 1912. page 420.

10 Clark, S. J. Record of Fairfield County: A Biographical Record of Fairfield County, Ohio.New York, NY: S.J. Clark Publishing, 1902. page 478.

11 Gen. Thomas Ewing Injured, 1.

12 Death of Gen. Thomas Ewing, 8.

13 Spencer, Joab. "The Methodist Episcopal Church, South, In Kansas--1854 To 1906." Collections of the Kansas State Historical Society. 1911-1912, Vol XII. Topeka, KS: State Printing Office, 1912. page 150.

14 Warner, Ezra J. Generals In Blue: Lives of the Union Commanders. Baton Rouge, LA: Louisiana State University Press, 1964. page 147

CHAPTER XI

WHERE WAS THE MISTAKE?

Many events occurred during General Thomas Ewing's life that one could cite as being mistakes. First, he resigned from the elected position as Chief Justice of the Kansas Supreme Court. Second, he joined the military and returned to Kansas as a brigadier-general. Next, he issued Order Number 11. Fourth, he defended three men during a politically charged trial, after which he supported a hated President and condemned the leading party's Reconstruction efforts. Finally, he failed to unify his party when he sought election. Any of these actions could become part of a game of supposition. Even his defense of Pilot Knob makes an interesting discussion topic. There are two main questions which should be answered. Did General Thomas Ewing make an overwhelming mistake? What legacy did he leave that no one else could have accomplished?

General Ewing made one mistake which could have been corrected at various times in his life; yet, he never made the effort. This decision proved to be the overwhelming error if he truly desired to be a US Senator. He left Kansas and never returned to stay after the war. When he became a general, he was reassigned to the Kansas District. He knowingly accepted the Border command in an effort to be close to his business interests, but that was a problem. He could not possibly appease both Missourians and Kansans; therefore, he was in a no-win situation. When Quantrill attacked Lawrence, he had to institute Order Number 11 to prevent retaliation from Kansans. It would have been politically better for him to have served elsewhere; away from Lane and Kansas politics, away from guerrillas, and, instead, fighting Confederate regulars. This position is exemplified by his service in the Saint Louis District, which few ever criticize.

After the war, his business interests were in shambles, but he did not return to Kansas. Instead, he moved to Washington to straighten out his monetary problems. True, Lane did not want him back, but Lane would soon kill himself. The Governor probably would not have appointed him to complete Lane's term, but Ewing would have been in position to challenge Pomeroy at a later date. No public office would have been far from his reach, for if there was one electorate which viewed Order Number 11 positively, it was Kansans. The only adversities Ewing could expect in the Sunflower State were due to his support of President Johnson and his anti-Reconstruction stance.

Becoming a Democrat limited his opportunities in that Radical Republican state as well. Surely he would have been a leader of the Democracy, as evidenced by the fact that some considered him Vice-Presidential material in 1868. As a Democrat, he may have always been defeated in Kansas, but he would have been a patriarchal figure in that party. If being a politician was his true desire, he should have returned to Kansas after his stay in Washington.

The Honorable Thomas Ewing, Jr., had two desires stronger than that of being a politician. He desired to be known as a successful, deal-making businessman with all the wealth associated with that success. Money was a major driving force for the General, but there was one greater. Several times in his career he set aside his avarice for that one desire he held above all others, preserving the Constitution, as he understood it.

Young Tom learned from his father and, presumably, his father's two friends, Webster and Clay, that the Constitution always needed to be protected. One way to protect it was through political office and that, most likely, drove his political ambition. Even when a personal benefit was not immediately forthcoming, Thomas Ewing, Jr., would step into the arena to battle those who would attempt to destroy it. He organized the bolters in Kansas and forced the rest of the Free Soil party to follow their lead. Without this act, the convention was doomed to failure, as they had already decided to boycott the next election which only would have benefited slavery proponents.

Ewing's Kansas business deals initially pleased both entrepreneurs and the Native Americans. Masterfully acting as both attorney for the railroad and the Kansas Indian tribes, Ewing obtained the lands he needed for his railroads. He developed the outline, which others later used, to obtain those Indian lands peaceably. Had it not been for Ewing developing this procedure, the bloody, forced removal of natives under Governor Samuel Crawford may have started eight years earlier. Imagine the federal government moving large numbers of soldiers into Kansas to fight the natives when those same troops were needed for a battle at Gettysburg. The name Thomas Ewing, Jr., is definitely one every Kansas child should learn.

Missourians should well learn his name, too. People vacated western Missouri because of Order Number 11, but the claims that it took those counties years to recover do not withstand the information provided by the 1870 census. The negative effects of his order caused suffering to the grandmother of a later President. Harry S. Truman was weaned on the stories of uncontrolled Bluecoat and Red Leg terror. President Truman later demanded complete obedience from his military commanders and promptly fired General Douglas MacArthur when the General violated his directives during the Korean War.

Ewing's stand at Fort Davidson saved Saint Louis and Jefferson City, which prevented a lengthening of the war. It also prevented the rebels from returning a Confederate government to Missouri (although most historians would agree

Price's idea of seizing total power in Missouri was fanciful at best). Had Price's Raid succeeded in its entirety, it could have cost thousands of lives, millions of dollars, and caused Missouri to secede from the Union. Secession could have changed Missouri history dramatically, as Reconstruction might have then been imposed on the state. While many might argue that few Union soldiers did more to hurt Missourians during the war, he easily redeemed himself in the autumn of 1864.

Samuel Mudd was spared from the noose and later pardoned because of the General's efforts. To this day, both Mudd's and Ewing's descendants continue the constitutional battle to reverse the Hunter Commission decision. He certainly sacrificed his personal finances to protect the office of the President and may have influenced the final impeachment vote. Ewing was finally elected to Congress and served two terms during which he fought against the stationing of federal troops at local polling places and shaped the monetary policy of the country. By the end of his second term, the Radical Republican influence was waning, and his best chances for higher political office had passed.

The Honorable Thomas Ewing, Jr., could have accomplished every major deed in his life which preserved the United States and its Constitution and still could have returned to Kansas for a more splendid political career, but he did not. The General could have boasted of his military successes, but he never did. Being the savior of Saint Louis certainly would have influenced any voters that "Order No. 11" propaganda may have swayed, but the absence of any reference to his wartime successes in his speeches proves that bragging was not in his nature. General Ewing's biggest mistake was not returning to Kansas for a political career while his name was still a household word. In the 1870s, he reached for a political career, but failed to obtain the office he desired. Then, he forsook politics of his own volition. Business was more important to Ewing than political office, but service to his country, even if it did not involve a political office, was of overall importance. His role in American history was controversial at times, but was so often pivotal that it is truly shameful that his legacy rests largely on historians' acceptance of the Bingham propaganda, which falsely records his political demise. Instead, he should always be remembered for his defenses of Doctor Mudd, President Johnson, and Pilot Knob.

APPENDIX A

GENERAL ORDERS NUMBERS 10 & 11

General Order Number 10

General Orders # 10
Hdqrs. District of the Border,
Kansas City, MO., August 18, 1863.

I. Officers commanding companies and detachments, will give escort and subsistence, as far as practicable, through that part of Missouri included in this District, to all loyal free persons desiring to remove to the State of Kansas or to permanent military stations in Missouri--including all persons who have been ascertained, in the manner provided in General Order No. 9 of this District, to have slaves of persons engaged in aiding the rebellion since July 17, 1862. Where necessary, the teams of persons who have aided the rebellion since September 23, 1862, will be taken to help such removal and after being used for that purpose, will be turned over to the officer commanding the nearest military station, who will at once report them to the Assistant Provost Marshal, or to the District Provost Marshal, and hold them subject to his order.

II. Such officers will arrest, and send to the District Provost Marshal for punishment, all men (and all women, not heads of families) who willfully aid and encourage guerrillas; with a written statement of the names and residence of such persons and of the proof against them. They will discriminate as carefully as possible between those who are compelled by threats or fears to aid the rebels and those who aid them from disloyal motives.

The wives and children of known guerrillas, and also women who are heads of families and are willfully engaged in aiding guerrillas, will be notified by such officers to move out of this district and out of the State of Missouri forthwith. They will be permitted to take unmolested, their stock, provisions and household goods. If they fail to remove promptly they will be sent by such officers under escort to Kansas City for shipment South, with their clothes and such necessary household furniture and provisions as may be worth removing.

III.   Persons who have borne arms against the government and voluntarily lay them down and surrender themselves at a military station, will be sent under escort to the District Provost Marshal at the Head Quarters. Such persons will be banished with their families to such State or district out of this Department as the General Commanding the Department may direct, and will there remain exempt from other military punishment or account of their past disloyalty, but not exempt from civil trial for treason.

IV.   No officer or enlisted man, without special instructions from these Head Quarters will burn or destroy any buildings, fences, crops or other property. But all furnaces and fixtures of blacksmith shops in that part of Missouri included in this District, not at military stations, will be destroyed and the tools either removed to such stations or destroyed.

V.   Commanders of companies and detachments serving in Missouri will not allow persons not in the military service of the United States to accompany them on duty except when employed as guides, and will be held responsible for the good conduct of such men employed as guides and for their obedience to orders.

VI.   Officers and enlisted men belonging to regiments or companies, organized or unorganized, are prohibited going from Kansas to the District of Northern Missouri without written permission or order from these Head Quarters or from the Assistant Provost Marshal at Leavenworth City, or the Commanding Officer at Fort Leavenworth or some Officer commanding a military station in the District of Northern Missouri.

By order of Brigadier General Ewing

P. B. Plumb, Major and Chief of Staff
Source: OR 1-22/2: 460-461.

General Order Number 11

General Orders Hdqrs. District of the Border, No. 11. Kansas City, MO., August 25, 1863.

I. All persons living in Jackson, Cass, and Bates Counties, Missouri, and in that part of Vernon included in this district, except those living within 1 mile of the limits of Independence, Hickman's Mills, Pleasant Hill, and Harrisonville, and except those in that part of Kaw township, Jackson County, north of Brush Creek and west of the Big Blue, are hereby ordered to remove from their present places of residence within fifteen days from the date hereof. Those who, within that time, establish their loyalty to the satisfaction of the commanding officer of the military station nearest their present places of residence, will receive from him certificates stating the fact of their loyalty, and the names of the witnesses by whom it can be shown. All who receive such certificate will be permitted to remove to any military station in this district, or to any part of the State of Kansas, except the counties on the eastern borders of the State. All others shall remove out of this district. Officers commanding companies and detachments serving in the counties named, will see that this paragraph is promptly obeyed.

II. All grain and hay in the field or under shelter in the district from which the inhabitants are required to remove within reach of military stations, after the 9th day of September next, will be taken to such stations and turned over to the proper officers there, and report of the amount so turned over made to district headquarters, specifying the names of all loyal owners and the amount of such produce taken from them. All grain and hay found in such district after the 9th day of September next not convenient to such stations will be destroyed.

III. The provisions of General Orders, No. 10, from these headquarters will be at once vigorously executed by officers commanding in the parts of the district and at the stations not subject to the operation of Paragraph 1 of this order, and especially in the towns of Independence, Westport, and Kansas City.

IV. Paragraph III, General Orders, No. 10, is revoked as to all who have borne arms against the Government in this district since the 21st day of August, 1863.

By order of Brigadier General Ewing:

H. Hannahs Acting Assistant Adjutant General.

Source: OR 1-22/2: 473

APPENDIX B

THE EFFECT OF ORDERS NUMBER TEN AND ELEVEN ON BATES, CASS, JACKSON, AND VERNON COUNTIES

While researching this book, an interesting piece of information was found in Steve Cottrell's The Battle of Carthage and Carthage in the Civil War. As the war progressed, the county population, which was 6,883 in the 1860 census, steadily declined to only 30 people in "December, 1865 more than half a year after the war ended."[1] Thirty represents 0.0044 percent of the pre-war population, a 99.99 percent reduction. The county in question is Jasper, which is on the western border of Missouri with Kansas. It, too, was a border county, but about forty-five miles below the area affected by Orders 10 and 11. It had one major battle fought within its boundaries early in the war. Additionally county records report fifteen skirmishes and the so-called "Second Battle of Carthage."

The second Carthage battle occurred on October 18, 1863 and started because Confederate Major Pickler failed to post pickets in Carthage the previous night. Early in the morning Colonel Shelby awoke to cannon fire. General Ewing, who had to spend time pursuing Shelby instead of chasing guerrillas, had attacked. Caught by surprise, Shelby rallied and positioned his forces to fight a delaying action while his main force retreated. The battle continued for about an hour, during which time Shelby escaped and Ewing's forces captured Major Pickler and 30 men. This was the last major battle in Jasper County, but, the following year, guerrillas burned down Carthage.

Jasper County suffered as a result of the normal course of the war. Carthage, like the county seats in several Border counties, was destroyed; however, it did not suffer greatly from the pre-Civil War border conflicts. The tier of counties from Cass down to Jasper all appear to have equally suffered from the effects of the Civil War, despite the fact that Barton and Jasper counties were not in the area commanded by Ewing. If massive depopulation occurred without Orders 10 and 11 in Jasper County, could this model be applied to the Border District displaced by Order Number 11 and a reasonable estimate of the people affected be derived there from?

The question of how many people were displaced by the Order has been answered in many ways, but almost always exaggerated. General Ewing stated that he drove two or three hundred families from the area. Some reports from those ejected from the Border indicated that the numbers were between 20,000 and 100,000.[2] Considering Jasper County's situation, as well as the fact that only about one-fourth of Vernon County was depopulated (instead of the one half often claimed), the claims appear to be Confederate or copperhead propaganda.

Before discussing the affected area more fully, one other point deserves consideration. The Jasper County situation also seems similar to the depopulated counties in another detail. Census records show that between 1860 and 1870, Jasper and all the depopulated counties nearly or more than doubled their populations, which was much faster growth than other areas of the state. The same holds true for Barton County, which is between Jasper and Vernon counties. Other counties north of the Missouri River along the Kansas-Missouri Border (Clay, Platte, Buchanan, and Andrew) did not experience this population growth; indeed, Platte County (which is directly above Kansas City, Missouri) suffered a decrease (table 1). So it seems that the situation in Jasper can be compared to that of the Border District and that a reasonable estimate of people removed by the Order can be made.

Information provided by the Missouri State Library (table 2) shows only 44,772 people in the four county area

196

during the 1860 census. This total includes all whites, free blacks, and slaves. That number definitely discounts the claim of 100,000 people being affected by Ewing's orders. Additionally, the order excluded certain areas (for example, three-quarters of Vernon County, and all residents inside or within a mile of Harrisonville, Pleasant Hill, Hickman's Mill, Independence, and Kansas City were not counted). Population figures for Hickman's Mill have not been located by this author. Hickman's Mill never incorporated and was merely a collection of houses near a mill. However, intensive research may yield an appropriate population figure. If the population figures of Kansas City (4,418), Independence (3,164), Harrisonville (675), Pleasant Hill (358), and three-quarters of Vernon County (3,638) are removed from the census data, a total of 32,519 people remained.[3] If Jasper County is indicative and Cottrell's source is correct in stating that the decline was steady, a twenty-five percent population loss each year can be estimated over the four years of war (April 1861 to May 1865) or a loss of 8,130 people per year (2,032 people per quarter year). Therefore, for the two and one quarter years between the start of the war and initiating General Order Number Ten, 18,292 people (statistically) would have left the affected area, leaving 14, 227 people. The popular estimate of twenty thousand people injured by the Order now seems too high.

One other factor deserves consideration in this mind game. Starting in the fall of 1859 and continuing well into 1861, "the granddaddy of all Kansas droughts" struck Kansas.[4] Since weather does not recognize political boundaries, this most likely struck the residents in these four border counties as well. Losses were devastating in Kansas. Homesteaders moved on because there simply were no crops for food, only a plague of grasshoppers in 1860. So, between the time of census and the Civil War, how many people left as a result of this natural disaster? That would have stretched the steady decline over a five year period from 1860 through 1865. Of 32,519 people in the census, 6,504 could have left each year during the years 1860 through 1862, with 3,252 leaving during 1863 before the orders. That totals 23,012 people, leaving 9,755 people in the affected area.[5] This figure is surprisingly close to the low number some people, such as Mark Grimsley, cite.

Should anyone plan to research this in the hope of providing the most definitive number that can be inferred from the remaining historical records, their research must attempt to answer some of the following questions, and must limit the count to those leaving after August 18, 1863.

First, the population of Hickman's Mill settlement would have to be calculated into the figures.

Second, the number of people who left between the census and the outbreak of war due to weather or the ongoing border wars would have to be determined.

Third, how many left to join either army and did not return prior to August 18, 1863?

Fourth, how many people moved into, were born, died naturally, or died through Red Leg or guerrilla actions prior to the orders?

Fifth, how many people voluntarily left their homes due to the ongoing war and skirmishes preceding the issuance of the orders?

Sixth, how many people voluntarily moved within one mile of Union Army posts because of continual border fighting and, therefore, became displaced within the counties before the orders took effect? Finally, how many Confederate soldiers returned to family life and did not become guerrillas prior to the Order?

General Ewing approximated that not more than 300 families were removed from the area due to the orders. If the average frontier family consisted of four people, he estimated that 1,200 people left their homes. What should be the number recorded in history books? The war was devastating, and, after the first year, the population should have fled to safer areas, such as nearby Union posts, or left the area entirely. Red Leg and guerrilla action was ongoing. Colonel Jennison created many of his monuments (as the standing chimneys sans buildings were called) before the orders. Likewise, many people on both sides had their animals, food, and possessions taken from them long before August 1863. Without food, animals, or possessions, many people should have left early in the war. Blaming General Ewing for the total devastation of the border, which started years before, is lazy research and accepts pro-rebel, pro-Bingham propaganda. Although the state stayed in the Union, Missourians have an extraordinary sympathy for the Lost Cause and its folklore. The numbers have always been a part of that propaganda, just as Harry S Truman's idea of the posts being concentration camps was a part. The projected numbers simply do not support 20,000 people, just as allowing people to move near a fort and set up housekeeping does not equate to the barbed wire of a Nazi concentration camp. Some group (as this research would - most likely take years otherwise) needs to research this much more fully. At present, with these statistical projections, history should record Ewing's estimate of 800 people as too low a number. This projection of 9,755 to 14,227 people seems highly probable, based on the Jasper County formula. However, it would not be surprising to find that the order displaced only three to five thousand people. Quite a difference from the historical claims.

Table # 1   Comparisons Table 1860 – 1870
Comparisons of Western Border 1860 – 1870 Census

Counties	1860 Census	1870 Census	Gain – Loss
Border County Districts			
Bates	7,215	15,980	+121.48%
Cass	9,794	19,296	+ 97.0 %
Jackson	22,913	55,041	+140.2%
Vernon	4,850	11,247	+131.89%
Other counties below Missouri River along Kansas Border			
Barton	1,817	5,087	+179.97%
Jasper	6,883	14,928	+116.88%
Counties above Missouri River along Kansas Border			
Andrew	11,850	15,137	+27.74%
Buchanan	23,861	35,109	+47.14%
Clay	13,023	15,564	+19.51
Platte	18,350	17,352	- 5.44%

Note: Newton and Holt counties also have a common border with Kansas, but were not included in this comparison as they share more of their border with other states. Holt (North of the Missouri) almost doubled its [population, while Newton, (south of the river) had a thirty-seven percent gain. Both reverse the trends of adjacent counties. Therefore, other growth factors probably are at work.[6]

Table # 2 - **1860 Population of the Missouri Border**
State of Missouri 1860 Census of Population

County	Townships	Free-Total	Slaves	Aggregate
Bates	Boone	771		771
	Charlotte	938		938
	Deer Creek	651		651
	Lone Oak	1011		1011
	Mingo	635		635
	Pleasant Gap	895		895
	Spruce	704		704
	Other (Note 1)	60		60
Totals		6773	442	7215
Cass	Big Creek	2008	233	2241
	Camp Branch	793	124	917
	Dolan	1771	145	1916
	Grand River	927	362	1289
	Harrisonville	675		675
	Sugar Creek	2097	1010	9794
Jackson	Blue	3611	863	4474
	Fort Osage	970	488	1458
	Independence	2486	678	3164
	Kansas City	4252	166	4418
	Sin-a-bar	1918	427	2345
	Westport	1061	134	1195
	Other (Note 1)	5859		5859
Totals		20,157	2756	22,913
Vernon	Center	758	60	818
	Clear Creek	421	13	434
	Deerfield	459	2	461
	Drywood	322	1	323
	Harrison	287	8	295
	Henry	453		453
	Little Osage	648	41	689
	Montville	1366	11	1377
Totals		4714	136	4850
All Counties		40,428	4344	44,772

Note: The totals of the Bates and Jackson show conflicting totals in the 1860 census document. When checked against the Population of States and Counties of the United States, still another was shown for Jackson County, but the same discrepancy for Bates County. As such, the differences were added to the table as other and under white/free-black aggregate. [7]

Appendix B Endnotes

1 Cottrell, Steve. <u>The Battle of Carthage and Carthage in the</u> <u>Civil War</u>. n.p., 1990. page 39.

    2 Eakin, Joanne Chiles. <u>Tears and Turmoil: Order Number 11</u>. Shawnee Mission, KS: Two Trails Genealogy, 1996. page 103.

    3 Meyer, Duane<u>. The Heritage of Missouri, A History</u>. Hazlewood, MO: State Publishing Co. 1970, page 242; Kennedy, Joseph C.G., <u>Population of the United States in 1860: Compiled from the</u> <u>original Returns of the Eighth Census, Under the Direction of the</u> <u>Secretary of the Interior</u>. Washington, D.C.: Government Printing Office, 1864, pgs. 288 – 291; Forstall, Richard L., ed. <u>Populations of</u> <u>States and Counties of the United States 1790 to 1990 (from the Twenty-</u> <u>one Decennial Censuses). Washington, D.C.: U.S. Department of</u> <u>Commerce, Bureau of Census, 1996.</u> pgs 93-96; Clatworthy, Thomas E.<u>,</u> <u>Cass County, Missouri 1860 Federal Census.</u> Harrisonville, MO: Cass County Historical Society, 1982, pgs 907-917; Group Vision 2020. City of Harrisonville Web Page: History. Kansas City, MO: nd, http://www.harrisonville.org/history.html Accessed 18 Nov. 1999.

    4. Castel, Albert. <u>Civil War Kansas: Reaping the Whirlwind</u>. Lawrence, KS: University Press of Kansas, 1997. page 14.

    5.   Shoemaker, Floyd C. <u>A History of Missouri and Missourians,</u> Columbia, MO; The Walter Ridgeway Publishing Co., 1922. page 229

Comment: After my research was finished I found a reference that of the 10,000 inhabitants of Cass County (1860 Census) only 600 remained after Order # 11. This is six-percent of its population. If this holds true for Jackson and Vernon counties (Bates had no population which could move near a post), the best figures for those removed by Order 11 would change to somewhat between 7,709 and 12,181 people. [wb 2004]

    6.   Forstall. Pages 93-96

    7.   Ibid, pgs 93-93; Kennedy, pgs 288—291

APPENDIX
C

UNLUCKY ORDERS NUMBERED ELEVEN

While the Order Number Eleven, discussed in this paper, is the most famous or infamous, two other orders with that number achieved notoriety during the Civil War. One was written by General Ulysses S. Grant and the other by Major-General David Hunter (remember the Mudd Trial and the Hunter Commission). Unlike Ewing's order, both created problems for President Lincoln and both generals were directed by the President to recall their orders.

In December, 1862, Grant was busy trying to take the river port of Vicksburg, Mississippi. Grant disliked war profiteering. As the Union armies headed south, Northern businessmen followed buying up anything (mainly cotton) they could find. Apparently, Jesse Root Grant, the General's father, was not aware of his son's feelings. He brought three businessmen, the Mack brothers, from Cincinnati, Ohio, down to visit his son. The Macks had offered him a share from cotton profits if Jesse would introduce them to his son in order to help them obtain the necessary business permits for the war zone. Upon learning of the reason for the trip, Grant had the Macks physically removed from the area. Unfortunately for Jesse, he did not count on his son's reaction. Even more unfortunate for the General, he vented his anger at the "race" of the businessmen instead of specifying profiteers . The Macks were Jewish.[1] Grant immediately issued the following General Order Number 11:

HDQRS. 13TH A. C., DEPT. OF THE TENN.,

Holly Springs, December 17, 1862.

The Jews, as a class violating every regulation of trade

established by the Treasury Department and also department [of the Army of Tennessee] orders, are hereby expelled from the department within twenty-four hours from the receipt of this order.

Post commanders will see that all of this class of people be furnished passes and required to leave, and any one returning after such notification will be arrested and held in confinement until an opportunity occurs of sending them out as prisoners, unless furnished with permit from headquarters.

No passes will be given these people to visit headquarters for the purpose of making personal application for trade permits.

By order of Maj. Gen. U.S. Grant:
JNO. A. RAWLINS, Assistant Adjutant-General.[2]

The order did not just affect Jewish businessmen. Any Jewish person within the boundaries of the Army of the Tennessee was to be expelled. Even more absurdly, the order did not specify that Jewish soldiers were exempt. When Jewish community leaders brought the order to the attention of President Lincoln, he directed that it be immediately revoked. Grant revoked it on January 24, 1863.[3]

While the main text of this paper has proven that General Ewing's Order Number 11 did not factor into his failure to receive the 1868 Vice-Presidential nomination, Grant's order did cause embarrassment during his election campaign efforts that year. Grant's supporters sought to blame other officers for issuing the order, but Grant admitted that he issued it, that it was not intended to cause suffering to the Jewish people as a class, but to profiteers, and that he was wrong.

Even though the orders of Ewing and Grant adversely affected people with in the boundaries of their military jurisdiction, Major-General David Hunter attempted to benefit people with his order and still caused President Lincoln problems. Hunter, a staunch abolitionist, had previously freed slaves in newly conquered rebel territories. He decided that since martial law existed in the areas under his command, he had the right to free the slaves in those domains. On May 9, 1862 , he issued his General Order Number 11. It stated:

HDQRS. DEPT. OF THE SOUTH,
Hilton Head, Port Royal, S.C., May 9, 1862.

The three States of Georgia, Florida, and South Carolina, comprising the Military Department of the South, having deliberately declared themselves no longer under the protection of the United States of America, and having taken up arms against said United States, it became a military necessity to declare martial law. This was accordingly done on the 25th day of April, 1862. Slavery and martial law in a free country are altogether incompatible; the persons in these three States, Georgia, Florida, and South Carolina, heretofore held as slaves, are therefore declared forever free.

By command of Maj. Gen. D. Hunter:
[ED. W. SMITH,]
Acting Assistant Adjutant-General.[4]

Kenneth Davis commented on President Lincoln's reaction, thus: "Lincoln still wanted this to be a war for the Union, not emancipation." Lincoln worried that if slaves in conquered territories were freed, the border states might secede. The task of preserving the Union and conquering the Southern states would then become more difficult. On May 19, 1862, President Lincoln overruled Hunter's order, and, in doing so, stated that he reserved that exercise of power for himself.[5] Seven months later, on January 1, 1863, Abraham Lincoln issued his own Emancipation Proclamation which announced that slaves "...within any State, or designated part of a State, the people whereof shall then be in rebellion against the United States, shall be then, thenceforth and forever free..."[6]

All three General Order Numbers Eleven created

issues for President Lincoln. Out of these, the President only endorsed General Ewing's order. On October 1, 1863, the Great Emancipator wrote: "With the matters of removing the inhabitants of certain counties en masse; and of removing certain individuals from time to time, who are supposed to be mischievous, I am not now interfering, but am leaving to your own discretion." Neely commented that this was because "after 1861 Missouri was largely irrelevant to the fate of the Union."[7] More importantly, Ewing's order dealt with legitimate military concerns. In contrast, these two other Order Numbers Eleven dipped into political affairs which created embarrassments for the President.

Appendix D Endnotes

1 Lutz, Stephen D. "Grant's Ignoble Act." America's Civil War Vol. 12 No. 6: (Mar. 2000): 50-56. Leesburg, VA: Primedia Special Interest Publications, page 50-54.

2 Official Records. The Civil War CD-ROM: The War of the Rebellion: A Compilation of the Official Records of the Union and Confederate Armies. Version 1.5 CD-ROM. Carmel, IN: Guild Press, 1996. Citation: 1-28/2, 424.

3 Lutz, 56.

4 OR 1-14, 341.

5 Davis, Kenneth C. Don't Know Much About The Civil War: Everything You Need To Know About America's Greatest Conflict But Never Learned. New York, NY: William Morrow and Company, Inc., 1996. page 243.

6 K. Davis, 274.

7 Neely, Mark E. Jr. The Last Best Hope of Earth: Abraham Lincoln and the Promise of America. Cambridge, Massachusetts: 1993. page 76.

APPENDIX
D

GENERAL EWING SPEAKS ABOUT PILOT KNOB.

General Ewing never wrote much about the Battle of Pilot Knob. His gallant service, except for Order No. 11, was never really questioned and did help him achieve certain goals in life. In his *Cosmospolitan* article about the struggle in Kansas, he mentions Pilot Knob, with regards to meeting Lt. Col. L. A. McLean (who he swore out a warrant against six years before) but otherwise is silent on the battle. Cyrus Peterson, when compiling the data for his book, does not record any information from General Ewing, but does so from Colonel Fletcher. This speech written by a *Missouri Republican* newspaper reporter records the General's comments, at length, on the battle.

There are some missing words in the text below, which I could simply not identify due to the condition of the microfilms. The microfilm copy owned by Fort Davidson State Historic Site is in much better condition than the ones loaned out from the State Historical Society which can not truly pass as legible. The text, however, is presented for the first time in almost 140 years, despite some five illegible words.

From the Missouri Republican, 8 Oct 1864, page 3
column 3

Serenade to Gen. Ewing

LARGE CROWD IN ATTENDANCE
DEFENCE OF PILOT KNOB.
THE RETREAT TO ROLLA.
Price's Invasion of the State.

It having been announced that Brigadier-General Thomas Ewing, Jr., would be serenaded at his residence on Locust street, between Sixth and Seventh, a large crowd assembled last evening to do honor to that officer. Meeting with a number of ladies, officers and citizens in the parlor, Mayor Thomas addressed the General as follows:

I am a man of very few words, and if there were many to be said I couldn't say them. All that I can say is that I act quickly, and will, during this rebellion. Your friends have desired that this compliment should be paid to you and your officers to-night.

Lately we have organized of the exempts, 4,[100 ?] volunteers for the defence of the city of St. Louis. I will say to you that if every exempt was a Ewing, a Fletcher, a Murphy, or a Williams, and such persons as composed your staff, that I believe that it would not require any more force than the exempts to take care of St. Louis.

The loud cheering on the outside interrupted the Mayor's speech, and the General stepped out upon the balcony, was introduced to the immense gathering by Mayor Thomas, and addressed them as follows:

SPEECH OF GENERAL EWING.

Fellow Citizens: I acknowledge, in behalf of that

portion of my command which fought at Pilot Knob, this very handsome compliment, and tender to you and to the citizens of St. Louis their thanks for them.

Coming here with but a few of the officers of the command, I left the whole of it at Rolla, turning over to Gen. McNeil the men worn out with fighting and watching for the defence of that important post, and by taking them he was enabled to collect for duty an equal number of fresh men, who have now reached the front of the enemy before Jefferson City.

When those left at Rolla, now under the command of the gallant and unyielding Fletcher, shall hear of this warm greeting, it will cheer them and nerve them for newer efforts. I venture to say if Price attempts Rolla on his retreat South they will give him a warmer reception than he received at Pilot Knob. They learned there and on the retreat, and taught the enemy, too, some lessons in the "no surrender" theory of warfare, and I venture to say that every man of them though they doubtless regard it a rugged schooled philosophy, is prepared to act by that theory, and stand to it to the end.

I may be pardoned here in presenting in a brief moment the *point* that was to be made by the defence of Pilot Knob. It is a mistaken notion to suppose that the authorities ever expected to hold that point against the great army of Price. General Rosecrans had no right to be called upon or to expect to have to meet with his small and scattered forces the huge army with which Price is now invading this State. The army which was to have met Price, that was prepared for him, was upon the Arkansas, and the authorities here could not suppose that Price would be permitted to pass from the front of that army into the State of Missouri.

But it came. The forces under General Rosecrans were scattered throughout the whole State, and it was important to have a few days to collect it and to gather in the spare troops in the adjoining States. Pilot Knob was merely used to delay the march of Price for two or three days -- that was the whole value of that point -- that was the whole purpose that I had in going there, merely to beat back the surging billows of the invasion until the note of preparation could be sounded, and sufficient forces collected. It was never regarded as the best defensible against artillery, but merely against a cavalry or infantry force. It served the whole purpose. I had guns enough, ammunition enough, men enough to do anything I could have done at Pilot Knob. I accomplished the object -- delayed Price at least three days, and then led him for four or five days longer on a fruitless chase. Whatever may be thought of it, it cannot be charged to Gens. Rosecrans, Smith or anybody else, that by their withholding reinforcements or in any other way the effort [died ?] of its accomplishment. It really deserves, I think, the honorable notice that has been given it, for the battle itself was a fierce one. The fort lies, you all know, like a penny in the bottom of a saucer -- lying in a little round valley, surrounded and overhung by five mountains over five hundred feet in height from all sides of which it was commandable by artillery and by sharpshooters. With two-thirds of his forces, Price attempted the assault. You know the result -- not in any official form, but by the authentic rumors that have reached you. I may surely say that during the two days he lost in that struggle 1,[300 ?] men, and he got as the result of his trouble, not the splendid warehouse filled with Quartermaster's stores, not 100,000 rations that Colonel Haines sent down there, not the enormous magazine filled with shot and shell, but a heap of blackened ruins in the fort, and the hill-sides filled with his dead and groaning wounded. His ferocity sharpened by the retreat he started on the pursuit, and Providence, and artillery, and fast travelling, saved us. We marched towards Potosi. On reaching Caledonia, my advance met the advance of Shelby, who had been ordered down, I assert here publicly, with his guerilla friends under

211

Reeves and Freeman, to murder the garrison, if captured. We met his advance at Caledonia -- whipped it, and taking the alarm, turned off on the Rolla road.

Travelling though the darkness of night which was pitchy black, gave us a start, and them, instead of taking the direct road to Rolla, by taking a road which leads over the divide between the waters of the Courtois and the Huzzah, which road leads down into a mountain gorge on a line of retreat which saved us. We reached this mountain ridge where it was impossible to flank us. We had scarcely planted our feet upon it when they came yelling on our track. The ridge was one of the mountain spur of the Ozark range. As I looked out upon the [dun ?] heather of the mountain sides, and heard the enemy coming, I felt forcibly reminded of the stirring description of the chase in the Lady of the Lake:

> "*Yelled on the view the opening pack,*
>
> *Glen, rock and cavern paid them back,*
>
> [line misquoted from Walter Scott's text]
>
> *To many a mingled sound at once*
>
> *The awakening mountain gave response;*
>
> *The falcon from her cairn on high,*
>
> *Glimpsed on its rout a wandering eye,*
>
> [line misquoted]
>
> *Till, far beyond her piercing ken,*
>
> *The hurricane had swept the glen.*"

And when after reaching Harrison Station, and after three days and nights of toil, watching and fighting we eluded the enemy and made good our retreat to Rolla. I [felt ?] that Marmaduke and Shelby called back by Price like the [taffied ?] hounds.

"Back limped, with slow and crippled pace,
The sulky leaders of the chase;
Close to their master's side they pressed,
With drooping tail and humbled crest."

There was in that struggle, however, aside from the more stirring incidents of the fight and the pursuit, very peculiar marks. I had gathered into the fort the new companies of Fletcher's regiment, which had been raised down on the extreme border of Arkansas -- men who had sternly withstood the ravages and fierce assaults of civil war, but at last almost in despair, abandoning their families and little farms had joined the service for the purpose of aiding in finishing the fight. They were the men who in many a lively fray for the last three years had watered the bridle paths of that border with the blood of the murdering guerillas. They were the men who under the lead of Leper, Powers, McMurtry and other leaders had made that border fearful to the guerillas. They were in the first and opposed to them the guerilla bands of Freeman and Reeves. They had been fighting to the death for the last three years these very men. Hardly ever was there a beleaguered army opposed by an army composed of men animated with such intense hatred to them. Do you wonder that they stood on the parapet fighting as if each man was fighting for his very existence? Do you wonder that I never thought of surrendering them? I would have sullied myself to have suffered the idea to have entered my mind.

Men! Never was there a moment in that siege or in the retreat when I dreamed of giving up as long as I had a rifle or a sword to raise in resistance. (Cheers.) It might be said that I had a right to expect that my men would be treated as prisoners of war. No they would not have been. Look at the fate of Major Wilson, the soldier, the gentleman, the fearless, spotless Christian, taken by them in fair fight as he was at Pilot Knob, stripped of hat, coat, vest, shoes, stocking, and made to walk through their camp, jeered at and driven by those hell hounds he had been fighting. And now the rumor reaches us, too well, alas, authenticated, that he has been given over to Tim Reeves to be murdered. If he is, I hope that the memory of his peerless character and of his atrocious murder will rouse the authorities to a revenge so swift and terrible that henceforth these men will have to act as soldiers or on both sides the black flag will be raised.

Ah! gentlemen, you little know you who have lived here in quiet in St. Louis, the character of that loyal people. You little know the hardships these loyal men of Southeast Missouri have endured. When I have marched by their ruined farms, and have seen their wives and children, shoeless, half-starved, eking out their existence in loneliness, I have bowed down in spirit before the heroic patriotism of these men and worshiped it. None of us have made sacrifices -- no man whose family has been in security and beyond reach of the terrible hazards of war has made sacrifices compared to them. Honor them, reverence them, aid them. Do as much as you can to relieve them, and after all that, you who enjoy your quiet homes here, will not discharge one-tenth of your debt of gratitude to them.

There was another striking feature of that siege. Price brought with him the pretended Governor of Missouri, and Tom Fletcher, God bless him, [cheers] left the place where I had put him on duty at Cape Girardeau, without orders, knowing that his six companies were then at Pilot Knob, and that his presence would be of the utmost service to them, obeying that instinct of duty that shows the true soldier and the true man, came to Pilot Knob, and was the last man to get into the fort before the drawbridge was raised. His arrival reassured and made confident the loyal men of these border counties who had rallied to the service at his call. They felt that he was willing to take all risks which I called on them to take, and they looked to him as their trusted, reliable leader. He did his duty to them in the siege and on the march most nobly, and you cannot honor him too highly for it. I have no

214

doubt it is felt very much by both armies as if the Governorship of Missouri depended upon the contest between them. If General Price succeeds, or if his peace friends (cheers) succeed, you will doubtless have Reynolds for Governor and Legislators to make laws for you chosen from his armies. (Cries of "*Never,* " "*Never.*") That is what peace now means. That is what amnesty now means. That is what cessation of hostilities now means. All that Price asks is to be left alone. Why! he wanted peace there at Pilot Knob. He didn't want to fight us, and he didn't want us to fight him. Almost before the fighting had fairly commenced he sent in a flag of truce. We fought him one whole day to keep him out of the Arcadia Valley. At night he broke through our lines and got in. He filled it full with his large army in the night. Then in the morning the contest was for the gap between Shephard and Iron Mountain, leading into the valley where the fort was. I had placed on the nose of Shephard mountain a battalion of the 14th Iowa infantry, whose presence there, with Major Wilson with his cavalry, made it impracticable for the enemy to force the gap without great loss. He wanted to get artillery to bear on Wilson and those Iowa men. He wanted a little time and he sent in a flag of truce. I sent another section of artillery to Wilson, and ordered him to reply to the flag with canister. [Cheers.] Afterwards when he had forced the gap and got possession of the top of the mountain, their lines were being formed for the assault, and it was desirable to have our artillery stopped while he was marching down the valley, which our guns commanded, and then there appeared an enormous white flag. Above a large rock Marmaduke was sheltered marshalling his forces. We turned the artillery on the rock and scarred it thoroughly and the flag disappeared again. It was ungracious not to listen to him, for he certainly meant peace; but it occurred to me that he didn't mean to surrender to me, and I knew devilish well I didn't mean to surrender to him. The amnesty talk, the peace talk is a flag of truce dodge exactly. Had we received the first flag of truce he would have had his artillery in position so as to have shelled us out. Had we received his second flag he would have had his storming party at our counter-scarp before we would have been ready to open fire. This Western rebel army use the flag of truce in the field as infamously as Forrest did at Fort Pillow. In politics I don't pretend to talk about purposes, but I say the effect of flags of truce on our western fields and of proposed armistices are exactly the same.

No. The portion and destiny of Missouri is to be settled by fighting now, this fall, not by peace talk, and the loyal people, the men without distinction of party, who wish this monster expelled with violence and blood from this State, owe it to themselves to unite, form one solid, compact body through the State, take and hold possession of it, and expel from it the men who will not be loyal to it and to the general Government. [Cheers.]

Colonel Baker, Commander of the Post, being called for by the assembled multitude declined speaking, but proposed to the crowd that they should listen to Major Williams, of the 10th Kansas and Major Murphy, two of the heroes of Pilot Knob. Major Murphy was loudly called out, but as Col. Baker express it, the man who never ran from his foes, had this time deserted his friends. Major Williams appeared and asked to be excused from making a speech.

Chas. D. Drake Esq., proposed nine cheers for Billy Sherman, the hero of Atlanta, the former law partner of Gen. Ewing, and made a few remarks called out by the occasion.

At the conclusion of Mr. Drake's remarks, Col. Baker was again vociferously called for by the crowd. Col. B., for the second time during the evening, presented himself to the crowd. He could not imagine what in the world prompted the crowd of patriots to call upon him for a speech; the audience, however, seemed to be aware of the fact that he could entertain them, and were determined to hear him. His remarks were appropriate, and were received with the greatest enthusiasm. He was for exterminating the rebels from our midst -- driving them from the city and State. The primary cause of the present raid was the sympathy manifested for the rebels here and throughout Missouri. Price would never have come here, had it not been for the presence of sympatizers [sic] in our midst, who were desirous that he should again reoccupy the State. Compliments were paid to Gen. Ewing and his compatriots at Pilot Knob. Col. B. also indorsed the Monroe doctrine. He was in favor of the next war! When we get through with our little difficulty, he was in favor of redressing some slight grievances with England and France. England has laid herself under obligations to us on account of the interest taken by her in the breaking up our ocean marine and furnishing the enemy with boats and munitions of war, and France for her endeavor to establish upon the throne in Mexico a scion of the rotten house of Hapsburg. No foreign potentate should rule upon the shores of North America. God Almighty had established boundaries for this great Republic, bounded on all sides by oceans and peninsula and Canada would become a part and parcel of this Union. He hoped to see the day when Mexico and Canada would be attached to this Republic, enjoying the blessings of religious and political liberty.

Colonel Baker's remarks were pithy and eloquent and elicited round after round of applause. We regret our inability to furnish a verbatim report of his speech.

APPENDIX E

In Memoriam.
Thomas Ewing,
Brevet Major-General, U.S. Volunteers

The following is the text from the MOLLUS report of the death of General Thomas Ewing. This original copy as well as other speeches I've collected during this research are on file at Fort Davidson State Historic Site, on permanent loan.

Military Order of the Loyal Legion of the United States.

Headquarters Commandery of the State of New York.
New York, April 1ˢᵗ 1896

Circular No. 35
Series of 1895-96.
Whole No. 498.

In Memoriam.

Thomas Ewing,
Brevet Major-General, U.S. Volunteers.

Died at New York, N.Y., January 21ˢᵗ, 1896.

Military Order of the Loyal Legion of the United States,
Headquarters Commandery of the State of New York,
140 Nassau Street,
New York, April 1ˢᵗ, 1896.

At a stated meeting of this Commandery, held at Delmonico's, corner of Fifth Avenue and Twenty-sixth Street, the following was adopted as the report of the Committee appointed to draft resolutions relative to Companion Brevet Major-General Thomas Ewing, U S. Volunteers (Insignia No. 7459), who died at New York, N.Y., January 21ˢᵗ, 1896, aged 66 years.

Report.
General Ewing was born at Lancaster, Ohio, on August 7,

1829, and came from an ancestry distinguished alike in war and in peace. Along the paternal line were the Scotchmen, Findley Ewing, who was presented with a sword by William of Orange for gallant conduct at the siege of Londonderry, the Thomas Ewing who came to the New World in 1718, the eleven Ewings who fought in the Revolutionary War, including the grandfather of our late Companion, Lieutenant George Ewing, who enlisted in the 2d New Jersey Infantry in 1775, and was with Washington at Valley Forge, and served through that war, and Thomas Ewing, his father, who twice represented Ohion in the National Senate, was Secretary of the Treasury under William Henry Harrison and Secretary of the Interior under Taylor.

Such was the stock from which the boy Thomas Ewing came. From 1850 to 1854 he attended Brown University, receiving in 1860 the degree of M.A. He graduated from Cincinnati Law School in 1855, removed to Leavenworth, Kansas, in 1856, and formed a law partnership with the late General Wm. T. Sherman. At this time the "irrepressible conflict" had commenced in Kansas, between the free-state settlers on the one hand and the pro-slavery settlers and the border ruffians from Missouri on the other, brought about in a large measure by the repeal of the "Missouri Compromise" and the "Squatter Sovereignty Doctrine" of Stephen A. Douglas. General Ewing went into the struggle on the side of the free-state men. The pro-slavery territorial legislature had enacted a law providing for a constitutional convention, which met in September, 1857, formed the "Lecompton Constitution," and its submission to the people. It was declared adopted by the pro-slavery men, December 21, 1857. This constitution provided for an election January 4, 1858, of a legislature and officers for the new State. General Ewing went as a delegate to the free-state convention held in December, 1857, called to consider whether or not those opposed to slavery in the new State should take part in the election under the Lecompton Constitution; and, with others of the more moderate free-state members, he urged participation in the election; and, when outvoted in the convention, General Ewing, with only twelve others of the one hundred and twenty-nine members present, withdrew, organized and nominated a full State, legislative and county ticket for the whole territory, every man of whom was pledged, if elected, to vote for a new convention to frame a constitution forever prohibiting slavery in Kansas. Within the ten days before the election he and his associates canvassed every part of the territory, and in his work General Ewing spent every

219

dollar he possessed or could borrow.

John Calhoun, Buchanan's Surveyor General, made a final effort to defeat the majority of free-state votes by declaring the success of the pro-slavery ticket. And he started for Washington to lay the Lecompton Constitution before Congress and secure the admission of Kansas as a slave State. General Ewing then procured the appointment of a committee from the free-state territorial legislature, of which he was the head, to investigate the frauds and forgeries of the pro-slavery men. The work of this committee resulted in the finding of the original election returns hid in a candle box under the wood pile connected with Surveyor Calhoun's office, the indictment of L.A. McLane, Calhoun's chief clerk, and his associates for forgery and conspiracy, and their flight. General Ewing then went to Washington with a memorial from the free-state legislature and the proofs of the fraudulent election conducted under cover of the United States authorities, and aroused such indignation throughout the country that Buchanan and his party in Congress were constrained to abandon the bill for the admission of Kansas under the Lecompton Constitution. Two years later Kansas was admitted as a free State -- thanks to the courage and energy of Thomas Ewing.

At the first election under the new constitution he was chosen Chief Justice of the Supreme Court of Kansas. He brought to the position, though but thirty years of age, ripe scholarship, legal learning and a full knowledge of the many intricate questions growing out of the long struggle of the people of Kansas for free statehood.

When the War of the Rebellion broke out, Judge Ewing resigned from the Bench, recruited the Eleventh Kansas Infantry (subsequently the Eleventh Cavalry), and on September 15, 1862, was chosen its colonel. He served in the First Division of the Army of the Frontier, Department of Missouri, Arkansas and the Indian Territory, participating in the battles of Cane Hill, Prairie Grove and Van Buren. On March 13, 1863, he was promoted to Brigadier General of Volunteers, for gallant conduct at the battle of Prairie Grove. He commanded the District of the Border, comprising Kansas and the western portion of Missouri, from June, 1863, to February, 1864, and of Southeast Missouri in 1864. His service in this position was full of stirring incident, and was of inestimable value to the Union cause.

It was while he held this command that he issued the famous "Order No. 11," for which he was in some quarters severely criticised

[sic]. Western Missouri was then overrun with bands of guerrillas and outlaws under Quantrill and other raiding chiefs from Mississippi, who were committing arson, murder and flagrant outrages on innocent men, women and children in Missouri and Kansas. These desperadoes were sheltered, encouraged and supported by the inhabitants in the border counties of Missouri, and in order to stop their devilish expeditions, General Ewing, on August 25, 1863, issued his "General Order No. 11," directing the removal of all the inhabitants of these counties within his district, except those living in and near the principal towns. The loyal people were to remove into these towns or to the military stations, or go to the interior of Kansas-- all others were required to leave the district. All forage was to be brought into the stations or destroyed. The object was to cut off the aid and supplies which the guerrillas had habitually received from the disloyal people affected by the order.

Though the order was executed without unnecessary hardship, and under a liberal test of loyalty, it was very harshly criticised [sic] by secessionists and some Union men. But it had become a military necessity, and it immediately and almost wholly stopped the devilish expeditions, under the guise of military movements, at which it was aimed. At that time murder and rapine were the constant employments of the rebel bands referred to, and no Union citizen was safe beyond the Federal military posts.

The sympathizers with these outlaws had often been warned against harboring and furnishing supplies to these guerrilla bands, and had defied these warnings and persisted in their course with the full knowledge that their Union neighbors were being murdered or driven from their homes by these cutthroats.

General Ewing finally, with the concurrence of General Schofield, determined to remove all of these people who proved to be sympathizers with the rebels; and at the time had under consideration the issuing of an order for that purpose, when the cowardly and infamous massacre at Lawrence, Kansas by Quantrill, of innocent men, women and children impelled General Ewing to issue his order at once in the form most effective to put a stop to this sort of butchery. It was a well considered and necessary order.

General Schofield in his official report, soon after the order was issued, says it was not done without the fullest examination and consideration by him; that it was not adopted hastily or as a consequence of the Lawrence massacre, and in his judgment it was wise and humane, and offered the first opportunity to the people in that section since the war began to openly show their attachment to the Union without fear of rebel vengeance. In a letter written since the war he says, "The responsibility of that order rests with President Lincoln, myself and General Ewing."

In September, 1864, the Confederate General Sterling Price, after long and careful preparation under the direction of the commander of the rebel trans-Mississippi Department, invaded Southeast Missouri from Arkansas with about 15,000 men, in three divisions, and constantly increasing his forces by recruits and conscriptions, advanced upon St. Louis, which was then defended by only a small garrison. The hope of the rebels and the fear of the Unionists was that St. Louis might be captured, and the whole State of Missouri go over to the rebel government. At the urgent request of General Ewing, General Rosecrans, commanding the Department, reluctantly permitted him to leave St. Louis and take command of Fort Davidson, near Pilot Knob, ninety miles from St. Louis, to make a stand there, and, if possible, delay Price until St. Louis could be reinforced and intrenched. In the fort were large supplies of ordnance and commissary and quartermaster stores, but the only men available were some odd companies from a few Missouri and Iowa regiments, some militia, the detailed soldiers and employees of the supply departments and the few remaining citizens, the whole not exceeding 1,100.

General Ewing reached Pilot Knob in the evening of September 26, only a few hours ahead of Price, and spent the night in organizing his incongruous command, and making dispositions to hold the fort. Price assaulted at daylight with one division, and later with two, aided by his artillery, which maintained a plunging fire from hillsides overlooking the fort, while he sent his third division to Mineral Point, in Ewing's rear, to cut the railroad, intending to capture the whole of Ewing's force. But this splendid soldier held his post with the most determined spirit for two days, successfully repulsing repeated assaults, and inflicting such loss upon the enemy that their dead and wounded found on the field actually exceeded in number the whole of his command. But he realized the precarious position of his brave little band, and under cover of night he evacuated the fort, blew up the magazines, and with all his men and field guns, marched toward Rolla, a fortified camp one hundred miles westward, fighting four days and nights with Price's third division on flank and rear. But he kept his command steadily in hand, and reached Rolla October 2, the survivors exhausted by the tremendous strain, and many

222

wounded, but all heroes. He had delayed Price a full week, compelled him to abandon the attack upon St. Louis, and set a glorious example to the other Union soldiers who soon afterward defeated and routed Price and drove him from the State.

General Ewing's loss in all the fighting, including the retreat, was 350 men, while Price's loss was fully 1,500.

General Rosecrans, in a special order issued October 6, 1864, says of this brilliant achievement: "With pride and pleasure the Commanding General notices the gallant conduct of Brigadier-General Thomas Ewing, Jr., and his command in the defense of Pilot Knob, and in the subsequent retreat to Rolla. With scarcely one thousand effective men they repulsed the attacks of Price's invading army and successfully retreated with their battery a distance of one hundred miles, in the face of a pursuing and assailing cavalry force of five times their number. General Ewing and his subordinates have deserved well of their country. Under such commanders Federal troops should always march to victory."

General Ewing resigned his commission February 23, 1865, at the close of the war in the West. On March 13, 1865, he was breveted Major General of Volunteers for meritorious conduct at Pilot Knob. After the war he resumed the practice of law, at Washington, with success. In 1870 he returned to Ohio, his native State, served as a member of the Constitutional Convention of 1873-74, and served from 1877 to 1881 with signal ability in Congress. In 1879 he was the Democratic candidate for Governor of the State. In 1882 he removed to New York City, where he continued the practice of his profession, until the sad accident resulting in his death, January 21, 1896.

He was a man of strong brain and of wide culture and learning. He was eloquent, polished and forceful with tongue and pen. Of him it might justly be said, as was said of his father before him: "He was stately and superb. His speeches were as dignified as his person was erect and noble. He was like a Roman senator in the gravity of his discourse and the decorum of his style."

In nature and manner he was kindly, winning and courtly. He was clean and pure of lie, honest in thought and deed. He was a lover of liberty and a friend of freedom. He was in closer touch and sympathy with all the good and plain people of the land, and had quick comprehension and keen intuitions as to their motives, purposes and needs. He loved them, and all who knew him loved him. Of him, as one of old, it may well be said, "The whole earth is

the funeral monument of those who live a noble life; their epitaph is graven not on stone, but on the hearts of
men."

Therefore, Resolved, That the New York Commandery of the Military Order of the Loyal Legion of the United States, by the death of Brevet Major-General Thomas Ewing, has lost a loved and noble Companion of the Order, a brave man, a brilliant officer, an able lawyer, a learned judge and a statesman eminent alike in the councils of the Nation and the States of his adoption.

Resolved, That this Commandery extend to his widow and children their profound and heartfelt sympathy in their great bereavement.

Resolved, That a copy of these resolutions, the report of the Committee, and the action of this Commandery thereon, be attested by the signature of the Recorder, and presented to the widow and family of the deceased Companion.

HENRY L. BURNETT,
Brevet Brigadier-General, U.S.V.}
JOSEPH POOL,
Brevet Lieutenant-Colonel, U.S.V.} *Committee.*
WILLIAM F. SCOTT,
First Lieutenant, U.S.V.}

By Order of Brevet Brigadier-General Horace Porter, late U.S.A., *Commander.*

A. NOEL BLAKEMAN,

Acting Assistant Paymaster, late U.S. Navy, Recorder.
OFFICIAL. Recorder.

INDEX